Christian Cyberspace Companion

A Guide to the Internet and Christian Online Resources

Jason D. Baker

Foreword by Steve Hewitt

Baker Books

A Division of Baker Book House Co
Grand Rapids, Michigan 49516

Published by Baker Books
a division of Baker Book House Company
P.O. Box 6287, Grand Rapids, MI 49516-6287

Third printing, March 1996

Printed in the United States of America

Library of Congress Cataloging-in-Publication Data

Baker, Jason D.
    Christian cyberspace companion : a guide to the internet and Christian online resources / Jason D. Baker.
        p.   cm.
    ISBN 0-8010-5248-3 (paper)
    1. Christianity—Computer network resources—Handbooks, manuals, etc.
    2. Theology—Computer network resources—Handbooks, manuals, etc.
    3. Pastoral theology—Computer network resources—Handbooks, manuals, etc.
    4. Bible—Computer network resources—Handbooks, manuals, etc. 5. Internet (Computer network)—Handbooks, manuals, etc. I. Title.
    BR99.B35   1995
    004.6'0242—dc20   95-6936

To Julianne

My wife
My lover
My very best friend

Thanks for walking step by step with me

Contents

- -

- -

Appendixes

A Parental Guidance Suggested   165

B Christian BBS List   169
C Christian Internet Directory   175

Glossary of Cyberspace Terms   205

List of Figures

Foreword

I can still remember my first computer. It had 16K of memory, used little square buttons for a keyboard, loaded programs with a cassette player, and had to run off our only TV, which served as a monitor. I also remember the first modem I connected to that poor excuse (by today's standards) of a computer. It ran at 300 baud. I was fascinated by the ability to log into other computer BBSs. This all took place in the late '70s.

Little did I realize then where it would all lead, and only in my wildest dreams can I imagine where it is going to end. With today's technology and the ability to travel in cyberspace, the door is wide open for Christians to go anywhere in the world, without leaving their own home or church. We can minister, explore, research, and even share the gospel message with millions as a result of the availability of telecommunications.

Christians many years ago were leaders in the technology of their day. We invented the printing press in order to mass produce the Bible. Most medical facilities and hospitals were started by the Christians of past generations. The same can be said for most schools of higher education. However, during the last few generations, the church has fallen behind. While the world embraced the introduction of the PC, Christians and churches were fearful, and viewed this electronic tool as a personality with a dark soul. Only recently have we caught up. Now, Christian homes, churches, and ministries have accepted the computer as a vital tool for ministry. Better yet, in the area of cyberspace, we have ceased to lag behind, and are even leading the way in some areas. As we shift deeper into an information age with the Internet, online services, and BBS networks, Christians should be leading the way. We have the greatest news of all, and should have the greatest burden to share it. The world is waiting to hear from us. Telecommunications has opened the door for us to accomplish this task.

Cyberspace is not the same as mass communication. It allows one the opportunity to speak as though to one person, and yet reach millions. It allows us to open the doors of our church electronically, twenty-four hours a day, to those seeking solace or comfort. However, cyberspace does have its pitfalls. There are those waiting to attack and flame. Yet, this new technology is opening new avenues for us to travel. Cyberspace may be the final chapter in providing us a way to fulfill God's command to GO.

Steve Hewitt
Editor-in-Chief
Christian Computing Magazine

Acknowledgments

Although my name is on the cover, many people have contributed to the development of this book. Unfortunately, I can't possibly list everyone who offered assistance, information, or encouragement, but some people deserve special recognition:

Paul Engle, my editor at Baker Book House. Thanks for giving me the opportunity to write this book and for patiently responding to my many phone calls.

Dan Knight, Mac guru at Baker Book House. I appreciate our e-mail correspondence during the course of this project; it added a personal touch.

Tom Podles, my supervisor at Loyola College. Thanks for allowing me to be flexible with my work schedule in order to finish on time.

Curt Crane, Todd Dworshak, Eric and Alice Molicki, Scott Radcliffe, and *Tom Wimsatt*, my volunteer editors. I can't imagine what this book would have looked like without you.

Laura Baker, my sister. Thank you for contributing your writing skills and encouraging words; both have been valuable.

My Honeymooners small group: *Tom & Stacey, John & Jennifer, Dave & Kim, Brian & Sheri*. Thanks for lifting me up with your prayers.

My parents, *George and Elsie Baker*. I am grateful for your constant support and encouragement.

Most importantly, my wife *Julianne*. You said back in college that I would write a book. This, however, was truly a team effort. Your encouraging words, meticulous editing, timely meals, writing breaks, perseverance, smiles, hugs, prayers, and love really made this book possible. You are a treasure from the Lord.

"Praise and glory and wisdom and thanks and honor and power and strength be to our God for ever and ever." *Soli Deo Gloria!*

I

The New Frontier

Throughout church history, Christians have witnessed numerous technological advancements. Some of these, such as movable type, have been well harnessed to produce great benefits for the church. Others, like television, have clearly been mixed blessings.

Welcome to the Information Age

In the last decade, the explosion of personal computers brought irrevocable changes to the way people work and play. Fortunately, pioneering Christians sought ways to employ this technology on the personal and corporate levels. Many churches now use computers to track membership and manage budget figures. Numerous believers use Bible study software to gain a better understanding of Scripture. Others have employed computers to play Bible games, create church newsletters, and aid in homeschooling. And now, more than ever before, Christians are discovering the benefits of computer communication.

Thanks to the National Information Infrastructure initiative, more people are discovering the world of cyberspace. Cyberspace is that realm where people communicate via computers and modems. Other terms used to describe this electronic community include online, network, and the ever-popular information superhighway. While cyberspace includes various bulletin boards and services, the most significant component is the Internet. The Internet, resembling an information flea market rather than a superhighway, is full of treasures such as electronic mail, online magazines, and discussion groups.

Why Go Online?

Cyberspace is a new world for Christians to explore. Imagine:

- corresponding with overseas missionaries without waiting days or weeks for your letters to arrive
- attending Bible college without ever leaving home
- discussing homeschooling resources with other parents across the country
- reading reviews of the latest Amy Grant or Steven Curtis Chapman albums
- participating in a worldwide discussion concerning worship styles and techniques
- searching multiple Bible translations electronically
- conversing with a Greek scholar about the use of the word *logos* in John's Gospel
- browsing the latest Christian magazines, such as *Christianity Today* and *Marriage Partnership*, without a subscription

These and many other experiences await you in cyberspace. Although many Christians have already started using the online world for personal growth and discipleship, millions more are missing some great opportunities. The online world is continuing to grow, and you have a real opportunity to not only witness history in the making, but to actively participate, and even influence, how cyberspace will develop in the coming years. Fortunately, some computer-savvy believers have already started harnessing the power of cyberspace for God's kingdom. As more Christians enter cyberspace, more resources will become available. In order for the church to take advantage of this extraordinary resource, Christians must learn how to navigate this online ocean.

Using This Book

This book is designed to introduce Christians to the online world with a particular emphasis on the Internet. You will learn what equipment you need, what services exist, and how to find your way around. *Christian Cyberspace Companion* is unique in that it includes a "Christian Internet Directory," a topical listing of Christian resources available online. This book attempts to meet the needs of new users as well as offer information to more experienced "Net surfers."

If you are a new user, you will find the bulk of the chapters full of information to help you become familiar with the online world. While this book is not intended to be the final word on the history or technical aspects of cyberspace, there is enough technical detail to give you an appreciation for the environment. Screen shots, tables, and examples are included to enhance your learning. Finally, each chapter suggests a few places to start exploring.

For the more experienced user, this book will serve as a handy reference guide. Chapter 2 condenses the entire book into a single chapter. By reviewing chapter 2, you can quickly refresh your Internet knowledge and then determine which of the subsequent chapters may further supplement your current understanding.

Some unique typesetting conventions are used in this book. Commands, address, and directories will look like this: `ftp kuyper.cs.pitt.edu`. Computer responses to such commands will look like this: `Enter Username`.

Before We Begin

The online world is an exciting place. As with most new situations, though, there is a fear of stepping into an unknown environment. Remember that all cyberspace users were newcomers at one time. In fact, the majority of cyberspace citizens have entered the community within the last few years. Most people online are friendly and more than willing to lend an electronic hand to new explorers. So don't be afraid to ask questions.

As with any journey, a good sense of adventure will go a long way. Fortunately, no matter what you do, you cannot "break" the various online services. Although you may see funny things on your computer screen, you will not cripple the Internet by typing an incorrect command. Have you ever noticed that children are not usually afraid of computers? They just start working with them and keep plugging away, regardless of accidents. Perhaps this is why many children are more computer-literate than their parents. So relax, experiment, play, try new things, wander down new paths, explore—the longer you spend in this strange new world, the more comfortable it will become.

While we're on the subject of children, it is important to be aware that cyberspace does have its dark side. Both pornography and child solicitation have found their way online. Appendix A addresses these hazards and provides some guidelines for concerned parents; these tips will help ensure that your journey, and your children's, will be educational and uplifting.

Despite the rapid advances during the past few years, the online world is still in its infancy. By going online, you have the opportunity to become part of the advancing information age. Contrary to much of the hype, we still have a long way to go before computers become as ubiquitous and easy to use as telephones.

Finally, love your electronic neighbor as yourself. The online world has a remarkable history of giving. People freely offer assistance to those they have never met and some even produce documents and software that can be distributed with little or no compensation. Continue in this tradition, and in the commands of Christ, by serving those you encounter. If you see someone who has fallen in a pit on the electronic path, stop and help that person up. Don't merely use cyberspace for your own gain. Be a giver and a contributor.

We have a tremendous opportunity to use cyberspace for God's glory, so what are we waiting for? Let's get started!

2

A Whirlwind Tour
of Cyberspace

While this book is intended to provide a detailed tour through the wonders of cyberspace, there may be those who are interested in getting a jump-start. In this chapter, we will explore all of the book's topics in an abbreviated format. The subsequent chapters will examine each aspect in greater depth. Because of the whirlwind nature of this chapter, many technical terms are not defined. You will find the various terms explained in their respective chapters and also in the glossary.

Essential Equipment

In order to go online, you will need a vehicle with which to navigate the information highway. Whether you prefer an IBM-compatible personal computer or an Apple Macintosh, you'll need to ensure that your system has the necessary equipment. The minimum requirements are a computer, modem, and communications software. A modem plugs into your computer and phone jack, enabling the computer to communicate over a phone line. While modems as slow as 2400 bits per second (bps) can work, 14,400 bps modems are recommended, especially if you are buying new. A general, all-purpose communications software package is needed so that your computer and modem can exchange information. If you are considering a new computer purchase, you can usually simplify the process by purchasing a multimedia machine.

Types of Online Services

The various online entities can be broken into five main groups: commercial online services, Internet connections through UNIX shell accounts, Internet connections through Serial Line Internet Protocol (SLIP) and Point to Point Protocol (PPP) accounts, Internet connections using proprietary software, and bulletin board systems. These five entities are the doors to cyberspace. Let's briefly look at each.

Commercial Online Services

The major players in the commercial online service industry are Prodigy, CompuServe, America Online, and Delphi. Christian online services, including Didax and OnePlace, are also available. The biggest advantage of commercial online services is that they are generally easy to use. Even for the beginner, America Online is so user-friendly you will wonder why you weren't online sooner. Furthermore, commercial online services offer a number of core features including electronic mail, encyclopedias, online magazines, and current news updates. For those interested in complete Internet access, online services are a mixed bag. While they offer many Internet features, most with graphical interfaces, they are often slower and more expensive than other options. Nevertheless, even Delphi makes accessing the Internet easier than most UNIX shell accounts. With their customized software and extensive member assistance, commercial services are the best places for new users to explore cyberspace. If you are more experienced or are primarily interested in the Internet, you may find a better alternative.

UNIX Shell Accounts

Much of the Internet consists of UNIX machines. It is only logical then, that a UNIX shell account is a good way to access the Internet. Essentially, you pay a provider a monthly charge in exchange for an account on a large UNIX system. This account gives you complete Internet access at a competitive price. Internet services and tools usually include e-mail (using Pine or Elm), USENET news groups (using Tin or Trn), FTP file transfers, Telnet, Gopher, and the World Wide Web (using Lynx). The advantage is that you get a lot of Internet access for little money. The disadvantage is that UNIX is designed for the power user, not the beginner. If you can handle a command-line interface and don't mind commands such as **ls**, **cd**, or **|more**, then a UNIX shell account is an economically sound choice.

SLIP/PPP Accounts

For more adventurous users, there are SLIP and PPP accounts. These are more expensive than UNIX shell accounts, but they allow you to dial in and actually be a participating computer on the Internet. Your computer will require some additional software to use a SLIP or PPP account. This software includes a Transmission Control Protocol/Internet Protocol (TCP/IP) stack, which, fortunately, has been bundled with the newest versions of various operating systems. Other useful software includes a mailer, newsreader, Telnet, FTP, and a Web browser such as Netscape. The ability to use Netscape or other graphical World Wide Web browser is the biggest draw for SLIP/PPP accounts. Although SLIP and PPP accounts were previously considered uncommon, their numbers are increasing and will probably continue to increase as Apple, IBM, and Microsoft develop their online services. Currently, configuring your computer for a SLIP or PPP connection can be quite a challenge; however, as more online features are incorporated into the operating systems, SLIP/PPP accounts may become as common as commercial online services. Regardless, such accounts provide you with maximum power for surfing the Internet.

Proprietary Internet Interfaces

The rise of online providers offering an Internet connection using a proprietary graphical interface is a recent phenomenon. Such interface software offers many of the same advantages of a SLIP/PPP account without the hassle of configuring a TCP/IP stack. The result is a graphical Internet connection providing all the major Internet services, often for less cost than a SLIP/PPP connection. These proprietary interfaces, such as Netcom's Netcruiser, provide a happy medium between the power of a SLIP account and the affordability of a UNIX shell account.

Christian Bulletin Board Systems

While not as in vogue as the Internet, Christian bulletin board systems are key resources for the believer. There are hundreds of Christian BBSs throughout the country. Many are run as ministries by computer-literate Christian system operators (Sysops). They are generally free and offer quite a few resources, including topical discussion groups, online documents, and programs for downloading. BBSs typically aren't as flashy as commercial online systems, but they are a great bargain. The opportunity to acquire free Bible study software, take theological classes online, or discuss apologetics with folks hundreds of miles away all for the cost of a phone call makes Christian BBSs worth examining.

The Internet

Considering that the Internet is over twenty years old, it is amazing to see the attention that it has been getting in the last few years. The Internet is actually the sum total of all computer systems that connect via a handful of central backbones. These backbones communicate together using the Transmission Control Protocol/Internet Protocol (TCP/IP) protocol. Unlike commercial systems, you don't actually subscribe to the Internet. Rather you gain access to a computer that is connected to the Internet and then take advantage of the numerous Internet services available to you. Over the Internet you can exchange mail with individuals from around the world, participate in thousands of topical discussions, download files, browse library card catalogs, and even view digitized photos and video clips. While nobody knows what form the information superhighway will take in the future, it is clear that the Internet will continue to be a valuable resource for years to come.

Electronic Mail

Probably the most common use of the Internet is electronic mail (e-mail) correspondence. Once you become familiar with addresses that look like **chris@christian.com** or **president@whitehouse.gov**, you will find e-mail a vital asset. Using an interface called a mailer, you can compose and send messages to people thousands of miles away. Best of all, they arrive at their destination within seconds or minutes of being sent. This instant communication is the beauty of electronic mail. You can also use e-mail to participate in topical discussions or to read informational documents simply by joining the appropriate mailing list. A wide range of resources is available, from the discussion of apologetics to an electronic magazine specializing in contemporary Christian music.

USENET

While some nostalgists lament the disappearance of the town hall or local pub, the Internet provides the opportunity to join in thousands of topical discussion groups via USENET. USENET newsgroups, also called Network News or Netnews, are hierarchical arrangements of discussion groups on virtually every topic under the sun. Using a newsreader you can choose to subscribe to the groups that interest you, read the latest postings, and post responses at your leisure. A number of newsreaders exist, including Tin and Trn for UNIX shell accounts as well as graphical readers found on Prodigy, America Online, and CompuServe. Christian newsgroups, such as `soc.religion.christian`, `rec.music.christian`, and `alt.music.amy-grant`, are excellent forums for questions, answers, opinions, and debates.

File Transfer Protocol

Yet another advantage of the Internet is that you have access to hundreds of thousands, if not millions, of files. These range from informational articles to digitized photographs to software programs that you can try before you decide to purchase them. You can retrieve these files by using the File Transfer Protocol, or FTP, service. Essentially you issue a command to FTP to a particular address, such as `ftp wuarchive.wustl.edu`, and you will log in to that particular computer so you can download files. Since nobody has accounts on every Internet computer, publicly accessible sites have been established so anyone using FTP can log in using the name anonymous. FTP can be a little tricky since you have to employ UNIX commands to move around, but the benefit is worth the struggle. Christian resources available through FTP include electronic Bibles, writings of the early church fathers, book and music reviews, and Bible games for children.

Telnet

Telnet is an Internet service that allows you to log in to a remote computer just as if you were local to it. Clearly this is useful if you have accounts on multiple computers since it enables you to log into them without having to make numerous phone calls. Telnet is also beneficial because some computers have been set up to allow the public to Telnet into them and acquire information. Two examples are `marvel.loc.gov` and `iclnet93.iclnet.org`. Telnetting to the first address will allow you to search the Library of Congress. Through the second you can visit the Institute for Christian Leadership's online system.

Gopher

Gopher is an example of a second-generation Internet tool. Rather than spending your time wrestling with cryptic UNIX commands or remembering Internet addresses, Gopher organizes information into a hierarchical menu system. Everything on Gopher is arranged in a menu form and permits links between computers. Ultimately Gopher servers are organized based on their geographic location. You can either jump directly to a Gopher page if you know its address, or more commonly, pick menu options that interest you and explore them. The beauty of Gopher is that the menu options may actually be located on different computers, but the Gopher software takes care of the addressing. Therefore, you can focus on the information you want, rather than where it is located. There are a number of Christian colleges and groups that have set up Gopher servers.

World Wide Web

The hottest second-generation Internet tool is called the World Wide Web (WWW). The Web organizes information based on a hypertext model. That is, you can jump from page to page based on key word links embedded within a document. It is much like the way that we often cross-reference in Bible study based on a particular word. Netscape is the leading graphical front-end interface to the Web, called a Web browser. Using Netscape you can surf the whole Internet without having to pay attention to addresses or specific locations. Furthermore, you can use Web browsers such as Netscape to perform other Internet tasks, like viewing Gopher servers and performing file transfers. In essence, Netscape is an all-purpose Internet interface. Netscape and the WWW are probably the most exciting things to happen to the Internet since its creation. In addition to the ease of Internet navigation, the Web also allows you to view pictures and video clips or listen to sound clips while online. With a Web browser you can spend hours cruising around the Internet without ever having to hit a single key—your mouse can take you everywhere by clicking on key words. UNIX shells often provide text-only Web browsers such as Lynx; some commercial online services and proprietary Internet software packages have customized graphical browsers; and Netscape is used over a SLIP or PPP connection. Numerous Christian Web pages exist, including ones focusing on the Dead Sea Scrolls, Christian musicians, creeds and confessions, and daily devotionals.

The Future

It is hard to say what the future holds for cyberspace. It seems that Netscape and other graphical interfaces will make the Internet even more accessible to beginners. As more companies offer online services and compete for customers, we can expect more features for less cost. It is likely that in the near future, using e-mail or having a personal Web page will be as common methods of communication as the telephone is today. This new realm will offer exciting new opportunities in evangelism, missions, and discipleship that we can only dream about today. The question is not *if* you are going to enter cyberspace, but *when.*

3

Essential Equipment

Just as you need a car to access an automotive superhighway, you need a vehicle to access the information superhighway. Many people believe that in the near future we will be accessing the online world with our television sets. Presently this is not the case. The personal computer is the current vehicle to travel online.

This chapter will present the necessary equipment for online travel. It is not designed to be the last word on computers or to endorse any particular brand of equipment. Nevertheless, it will provide an introduction to the essential equipment and terminology required for cyberspace access.

What Kind of Computer Do I Need?

Personal computers are similar to cars—there are numerous brands, confusing options, and they depreciate as soon as you take them home. As with cars, you should do some research before buying a personal computer. If you can find someone who is knowledgeable about computers, get their advice before making a purchase. Keep in mind that the sixteen-year-old who lives next door may be better equipped to offer advice than the professional down the street. Other good sources of information are magazines such as *Consumer Reports*, *Christian Computing*, *PC World*, and *Mac-World*. Often these magazines will run articles assisting new users with computer purchases.

Apple versus IBM

The first choice to be made is whether to purchase an Apple Macintosh or an IBM (or IBM-compatible) personal computer. This issue often sparks the kind of debates usually reserved for denominational battles. There is no right or wrong answer. In fact, with the widespread acceptance of Microsoft Windows in the PC (that is, IBM-compatible) world, Macs and PCs are becoming remarkably similar in their look and feel. Despite such similarities, the two computer platforms are not compatible. Since either type of computer will permit you to enter the online world, it boils down to a matter of taste. A good policy is to purchase the type of computer that you use at work or that your kids use at school. This will help shorten the learning curve.

Hardware Fundamentals

A personal computer fundamentally consists of a processor, Random Access Memory (RAM), disk drive(s), a monitor, and a keyboard. Common peripherals include a mouse, a sound card, a Compact Disc-Read Only Memory (CD-ROM) drive, and a printer. The one essential peripheral for entering cyberspace is a modem. Due to their importance, modems will be addressed in a separate section. Before focusing on specifics, let's understand what purpose each primary component serves.

The processor is the computer chip that serves as the engine of your computer. Historically, processors have carried numerical designations such as 80386, 80486, and 68040. Newer processors are receiving names such as the PowerPC and Pentium. As you might expect, the newer processors are faster and more powerful than their predecessors.

A computer's RAM is where information is stored while the processor performs the appropriate computations on it. In the same way that you might scrawl numbers on a notepad when doing a math problem, computers "write down" the data in RAM. RAM is sold in megabytes, which is simply a measure of capacity like gallons or liters. If you read an advertisement saying that a computer comes with 8 megs of memory, that is shorthand for saying 8 megabytes of RAM. As computer programs get more sophisticated, and processor-hungry, more RAM is required to effectively handle the larger quantities of information being manipulated.

The next major component of a computer is the hard disk or hard drive. A hard drive is a magnetic storage unit on which you keep software programs, data, and other information. The hard disk resides inside your computer's case and is generally not portable. This is in contrast to floppy disks, which allow you to physically transport software between computers. A hard drive's storage capacity is measured in megabytes. With larger drives becoming standard, the term *gigabyte*, about 1000 megabytes, is also common. Since software continues to require greater disk space, you would be wise to acquire a large hard drive when buying a computer.

The monitor and keyboard components are rather straightforward. A monitor is the visual part of your computer. Monitor resolution, stated in dot pitch, is a description of a monitor's crispness. Dot pitch measures the size of the dots that comprise a screen image. The smaller the dot pitch, the better the clarity. The keyboard is the primary interface between you and your computer. Keyboards come in different shapes and sizes, but the standard computer keyboard contains 101 keys.

Because the computer market changes so rapidly, it is impossible to suggest the perfect computer. There is always something bigger, faster, or better on the verge of production. A good philosophy when purchasing a computer is to purchase the best system that you can possibly afford. If you purchase an underpowered computer, you may not be able to run the latest programs. By spending the extra money you stand a greater chance of your computer serving you longer. With the rapid changes in the computer world, if you can get a computer to stay current for three or more years, you are doing very well. It's not that the computer will break or wear out; it's just that over time the new software will outstrip your existing hardware.

IBM PC Specifications

If you choose to purchase an IBM or compatible PC, you will be faced with a myriad of brands and options. As long as the vendor guarantees 100 percent IBM compatibility, it really doesn't matter whether you purchase a genuine IBM or a clone such as Gateway 2000, Dell, or Compaq. Regardless of whom you purchase your computer from, be sure to examine their warranty and support policies. Also, if you are new to computers, you should inquire about any training or assistance programs that may be offered. Typically, you will find computers cheaper if you purchase them using mail order; however, by buying from a local store you can try out the system before the sale, and you can also establish a local contact in case of problems.

Processor

Most PCs use processors that belong to the 80x86 family of chips developed by Intel. Rather than referring to a chip as an 80486, it is typically called a 486. The most common processors are the 286, 386, 486, and Pentium. When a computer is advertised as a Pentium, it simply means that the computer contains the Pentium processor chip. Processors run at different speeds, which are measured in megahertz. A megahertz, or MHz, is similar to the speed of a car measured in miles per hour, or mph. The greater the MHz value, the faster the computer runs.

If you currently own a computer with at least a 386 processor, you will have little trouble cruising through cyberspace. If you intend to buy a new computer, be sure to maximize your investment. While less powerful processors will be cheaper, they are not wise investments . You should strongly consider getting at least a 486 running at 33 MHz. If you can afford it, opt for a 100 MHz 486 or even a Pentium machine.

In an attempt to offer an alternative to Intel's processors, a joint venture between IBM, Apple, and Motorola resulted in a series of chips known as the PowerPC. While IBM has made many promises about designing PowerPC systems to compete with Pentium machines, they have been slow to bring systems to market. Since PowerPC computers may become a viable alternative to Pentium machines, they are also worth researching before making your purchase.

Memory

Because of increasing software requirements, you should purchase as much RAM as you can. As newer software is developed—especially software designed to run with Microsoft Windows—you will need greater amounts of RAM to run the programs. Twelve or even 16 megs of RAM are ideal. At a minimum you should purchase 8 megs of RAM. Anything less than 8 megs will not be adequate to run the latest software.

Hard Drive

Newer software doesn't just require more RAM; it also consumes more space on your hard drive. While a 40-megabyte hard drive was adequate only a few years ago, it isn't nearly enough today. Once again, the rule is to buy as much as you can afford. A hard drive of at least 350 megs is recommended.

Monitor

Since the online world is rapidly becoming a graphical environment, a poor monitor will hinder your cyberspace travel. Be sure to purchase a color monitor that is at least fourteen inches in the diagonal with a 0.28 dot pitch or less. In order to advertise a low price, some vendors will offer a computer system that comes with a 0.39 dot pitch monitor, so be wary of this.

Apple Macintosh Specifications

Unlike in the PC world, there are no Macintosh-compatible computers. If you decide to purchase a Mac, you will be buying directly from Apple. This eliminates much of the confusion and competition found in the IBM camp. Recently, however, Apple offered to license their technology to competitors in hopes of increasing Macintosh's market share. Mac clones will mark a significant change in the personal computer market.

Processor

The processors for Macs, historically developed by Motorola, have been part of their 680x0 line. Despite the different numbering schemes, the Motorola chips used in the Macs have paralleled the processing power of the Intel chips used in the IBM-compatibles. Thus the Mac 68040s are roughly equivalent in power to PCs with Intel 80486 chips. The new generation of Macintoshes are using PowerPC chips developed by Apple, Motorola, and IBM. These Power Macs compete with the Pentium and PowerPC computers in the IBM world.

Most Macs purchased in the last few years should be suitable for online exploration. If you are planning to purchase a new Macintosh, however, you should go no lower than a 68040 processor running at 25 MHz. Given Apple's push for their Power Macs, remaining inventories of 68040s have become very affordable (but also quite limited). Nevertheless, it is wiser to invest in a Power Mac if you can afford it.

Memory

You should purchase, at the very minimum, 8 megabytes of RAM with the 680x0 models and 12 megs with the Power Macs. If you buy a Power Mac, 16 megs is strongly recommended. The more memory you purchase, the better off you will be in the long run.

A big advantage of the Power Macs is that you can run software developed for both the Macintosh and Microsoft Windows platforms. By purchasing a Windows emulator package, such as SoftWindows, the Power

Mac can run Windows software that was previously only available for IBM-compatible machines.

Hard Drive

When it comes to hard drive capacity, 250 megabytes is the absolute minimum that you should purchase. As software increases in size, bigger hard drives become more significant. Fortunately, disk storage is rather inexpensive in comparison to other computer components, often costing less than one dollar per megabyte.

Monitor

Prospective Macintosh buyers are fortunate because Apple produces high-quality monitors. Unlike with IBM-compatibles, it is unlikely that a vendor will offer a poor monitor in a bargain package. Select at least a fourteen-inch color monitor, with no greater than 0.28 dot pitch.

Modems

A computer by itself is not capable of communicating with the online world. In order to access the Internet and other points in cyberspace, you will need to purchase a modem. The name *modem* actually stands for modulator-demodulator. Modems take the digital signals used by your computer and convert, or modulate, them into analog signals that can then be sent over a standard voice-grade telephone line.

Modems come in a variety of different shapes and sizes. Internal modems are mounted inside your computer. External modems reside outside of your computer's case. Either way, a modem plugs into your computer using a special cable or physical connection within the computer. By plugging your phone line into the modem you create a pipeline to the outside world.

Generally, modems are not computer specific. Although you cannot use an internal PC modem with a Mac, external modems can be interchanged. The only hardware difference is that an external modem for a PC requires something called an RS–232 serial cable, while the Mac requires a Mac modem cable. When you purchase your modem, be sure to request the cable for your specific computer.

Just as the majority of PCs are IBM-compatible, most modems are Hayes-compatible. Hayes, one of the original modem manufacturers, created a common set of commands to enable a computer to talk to a modem. Such commands include dialing, hanging up, and answering the phone. Check to ensure any modem that you purchase is Hayes-compatible, regardless of which hardware platform you purchase it for, because most modem software uses the Hayes standard.

The primary distinguishing factor among modems is the speed that they can transmit information over the phone line. This speed is measured in bits per second (bps); that is, the number of computer bits that the modem can transmit or receive in one second. Sometimes advertisements will incorrectly use the term *baud rate* instead of bps. Baud rate is a term that actually refers to a modem's transmission frequency rather than its throughput; therefore, be sure to look at bps when purchasing a modem.

Common rates include 2400, 9600, 14,400, and 28,800 bps. While modems as slow as 2400 bps can be used to navigate the online world, you should not purchase any modem with a bps rate less than 14,400 bps, otherwise referred to as 14.4K. Buying a 2400 bps modem today is like purchasing a car that can only go 25 miles per hour; it just isn't fast enough for highway driving. With newer 14.4K modems selling for under one hundred dollars, it isn't worth buying anything slower. Depending on their price, 28.8K modems may be a good choice. If you have the opportunity or need, consider purchasing a fax/modem. Fax/modems are unique because they can send and receive faxes using your computer. They are quickly becoming the standard.

Multimedia

Multimedia, or the use of video and sound on your computer, is currently a hot topic. Although not a necessity when purchasing a computer, you should consider buying a system with a CD-ROM drive, a sound card, and speakers. Newer features on commercial online services and the Internet allow you to listen to a variety of sounds and watch video clips. Furthermore, some services like CompuServe are starting to produce CD-ROMs that correspond with their online services and offer new features.

CD-ROM

CD-ROM drives have become very popular in the last few years and thus have fallen in price. If you buy a CD-ROM drive, ensure that it is at least a double-speed drive. If there is not much of a price difference, opt for a triple-speed drive. The faster the drive, the better the response time when running software. Speed is particularly noticeable when doing complex searches from a CD or playing video clips. If you have appropriate sound equipment, you can also use a CD-ROM drive to play regular audio CDs through your computer.

Sound

To enjoy sound clips, either online or from a CD-ROM, you will need to ensure that your computer is capable of handling sound. Macintoshes have always had good sound systems, so Mac users need only purchase speakers to enhance the sound quality. PCs, on the other hand, have poor sound capability and thus require a sound card. A 16-bit sound card that is Soundblaster-compatible is recommended. Soundblaster is currently the leading sound card; like Hayes modems, Soundblaster has established an industry standard. You will also need to purchase a set of speakers to accompany the sound card.

An Ideal System

Considering the options, it is best to purchase a multimedia computer. Many vendors, including Apple, IBM, and clone companies, package a computer with everything that you will need to run multimedia software. Typical computers will meet the aforementioned processor, memory, and hard drive specifications and will also include a modem, CD-ROM drive, sound card, and speakers. Not only will you get everything you need to go online and enjoy multimedia, but it is often cheaper than buying all of the various components separately. Furthermore, the vendor will probably pre-configure all of the software for you so you can just unpack the system, plug it in, and start working.

Operating Systems

A computer needs more than hardware to run; it also needs software called an operating system to tell the computer what to do. The operating system, or OS, is what you will interact with on a daily basis.

Macintosh

If you purchase a Macintosh, you will automatically receive the latest Macintosh operating system, denoted by a system number. Although

Apple is currently working on the next major release of the Mac operating system, expected to be System 8.0, the current version is System 7.5. The Mac OS is noted for its graphical interface, complete with icons and pull-down menus, and ease of use. Since Apple's System software is the only OS available when purchasing a Mac, you don't have to choose between competing products. If you currently have a Macintosh, it is advisable to upgrade to the latest version of the operating system in order to support the latest applications.

DOS

PC users, on the other hand, have a number of issues to confront. Since the creation of the original IBM PC, the operating system of choice has been DOS. DOS, or the Disk Operating System, is a text-based OS that comes with almost every PC machine sold. DOS is notoriously unfriendly and difficult for new users to use. Since it is currently on the overwhelming majority of IBM-compatibles, you can expect to find DOS bundled with most computer systems.

Windows

During the last few years Microsoft has popularized a software product called Windows, which runs on top of DOS and provides a graphical interface. Microsoft Windows resembles the Mac OS in that it uses icons, menus, and a pointing device called a mouse to navigate rather than typing commands. Windows 3.1 was the version that really convinced the majority of PC owners to go graphic. Windows 95 is the next generation of the Windows environment, which actually combines DOS and Windows into a complete operating system. This version allows the PC user to work totally in a graphical environment much like the Mac. If you have a computer that doesn't have the latest version of Windows, or any version of it, it's a good idea to purchase that software. All of the major online services, including most commercial systems and the Internet World Wide Web browser Netscape, are best seen with a graphical interface.

OS/2

Another option for PC users is IBM's second-generation operating system known as OS/2. The latest version, called OS/2 3.0 or OS/2 Warp, is a graphical alternative to DOS and Windows. Many of the features of OS/2 2.1 and 3.0 are similar to those in Windows 95. Despite the similarities, OS/2 has not gained the sizable user base that Windows has. While there are many aspects of OS/2 that make it a technically superior operating system, the simple fact is that the vast majority of PCs are sold with DOS and Windows. If you consider yourself adventurous or computer-literate, you would probably benefit from trying out OS/2. New users should stick with DOS and Windows simply because support and assistance are more readily available.

Operating Systems and the Internet

Fortunately, the latest versions of these operating systems have been specially designed for use with the Internet. In chapter 5 we will look at different types of connections to the Internet and explain what software is required for dial-up Internet connections. Such connections have been made significantly easier now that the operating systems have the appropriate communications software already built into them.

Communications Software

There are a number of software packages that are required when exploring the online world. Most of these packages will be discussed in later chapters. No cyberspace citizen can be without a standard communications package for simple online connections. Such software is either referred to as communications software or terminal emulation software.

A terminal emulator is a program that allows you to call and communicate with another computer using a modem. Such software is essential for calling bulletin board systems (BBSs), UNIX shell accounts, and other online systems that lack proprietary software. While some of the operating systems, including Windows and OS/2, have built-in communications software, they are usually lacking in some major features.

Most communications programs allow you to emulate both VT100 and ANSI terminals. VT100 is the most common terminal setting, which is actually a holdover from the days of using "dumb" terminals attached to mainframe computers. ANSI is a terminal setting that allows your computer to display special graphical characters. It is used by some BBSs to create intricate menus. Good communications packages will also provide a phone book so you can store phone numbers with their corresponding terminal settings.

Communications software also allows you to download and upload files. Downloading is when you transfer files from a remote computer to your computer, while uploading refers to sending files from your computer to a remote site. There are protocols that allow two computers to successfully transmit the files, most commonly Kermit, Xmodem, Ymodem, and Zmodem. You should look for communications software that supports all four of these.

When you buy a modem or a multimedia computer, try to get one with communications software included. Communication programs, such as Procomm and Delrina Communications Suite, can also be purchased commercially through stores or through mail order. Other products, such as Zterm for the Mac and Microlink for Windows PCs, are available online and can be downloaded from BBSs or commercial online services. A screen shot of Microlink for Windows is shown in figure 1.

If you don't have a good communications package, you may want to ask someone who has a similar computer if they have one that they can give you. While you cannot copy commercial software, shareware and freeware are types of software that can be duplicated. More information about shareware and freeware is found in chapter 11. Another cost-effective way of acquiring communications software is to download it from a BBS or online service. If your operating system came with a basic terminal emulator,

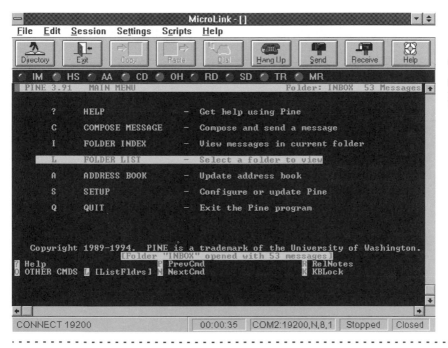

Figure I

Microlink
for
Windows

you can call a BBS and download a more advanced package. If, for some reason, you don't have any communications software and don't want to purchase a package at a software dealer, the easiest method is to call and order a free trial membership with a commercial online service such as America Online. When you do this, the online service will mail you a disk with their proprietary communications software. You can then connect to the commercial service, find a communications package in their software libraries, and download it for future use.

4

Commercial
Online Services

By now you're probably anxious to put your computer system to work and start traveling. As mentioned in chapter 2, there are five main categories of online services: commercial services, UNIX shell accounts, direct Internet connections using SLIP or PPP accounts, proprietary Internet interfaces, and computer bulletin board systems (BBSs). This chapter will focus solely on commercial services, chapter 5 will discuss the various Internet account types, and chapter 6 will give an introduction to Christian bulletin board systems.

Why Choose a Commercial Online Service?

Commercial online services combine a large amount of information with a user-friendly interface. Although these services have historically been self-sufficient, they are working feverishly to expand their Internet capabilities. We will focus on the four largest commercial online services: America Online, CompuServe, Delphi, and Prodigy. Two forthcoming Christian online services, Didax and OnePlace, will also be briefly introduced. Before examining each of these services in depth, let's take a quick look at what they all have in common.

Online services are like restaurants. Although restaurants differ in cuisine and style, they generally have some staple foods to satisfy everyone. Just as you can expect to find hamburgers on most restaurant menus, you will find features like e-mail and discussion groups on all of the online services. Other staples include current news information, business and financial references, educational material, electronic shopping, travel services, downloadable software, and games. As with restaurants, each online service adds its own flavor to the staple choices. For example, America Online offers users the ability to search *Compton's Encyclopedia,* while Delphi provides *Grolier's Encyclopedia.*

Which One Is the Best?

At this point many of you probably want to know which service is the best. This is a difficult and broad question, similar to asking which car is the best. As cars vary in performance, options, and prices so the different major online services vary in their features, ease of use, cost, and Christian resources. The following table compares the four major commercial services. Remember that all four services contain the staple features mentioned in the previous section. Note that functions like USENET, Gopher, Telnet, and FTP are Internet services and will be examined in greater detail in their respective chapters.

The best way to determine which of these commercial online services you prefer is to compare them yourself. Fortunately these services often

Service	America Online	CompuServe	Delphi	Prodigy
Subscribers	5 million	4 million	150,000	2.5 million
Supported Platforms	Windows, DOS, Mac	Windows, DOS, Mac	Windows, DOS, Mac	Windows, DOS, Mac
Navigation	Excellent	Very Good (Graphical), Good (Text)	Good	Very Good
Christian Discussion	Christianity Online, Religion and Ethics Forum	Christian Interactive Network (CIN), Religion Forum	Theological Network Group	Religion Concourse 1 and 2
Christian Files	Yes	Yes	Yes	Yes (limited)
Internet E-Mail	Yes	Yes	Yes	Yes
USENET Groups	Yes	Yes	Yes	Yes
FTP	Yes	Yes	Yes	Yes (using WWW)
Telnet	Yes	Yes	Yes	No
Gopher	Yes (limited)	Yes	Yes	Yes (using WWW)
World Wide Web	Yes	Yes	Yes (text only)	Yes
Base Cost	$9.95 per month	$9.95 per month (additional charge for some CIN features)	$10.00 per month	$9.95 per month

Figure 2

America
Online
Main Menu

advertise a free, or low-cost, trial period, so you can test drive without breaking your budget. Each of the following sections will provide a brief overview of a particular service (emphasizing its Christian content) and will also include information on how to contact the company for more information.

America Online

America Online, also known as AOL, has received much attention in the last year for being the fastest-growing commercial online service. It's no wonder, because AOL is by far the easiest of all of the systems to use. New organizations and services are appearing almost daily. America Online is pursuing an aggressive marketing strategy in an attempt to become the largest commercial online service. AOL's Windows, DOS, and Macintosh interfaces are all graphical and virtually identical. From the colorful icons to the "You Have Mail" voice that emanates from your computer when your mailbox is full, AOL is a friendly place. Figure 2 presents the opening screen from America Online.

America Online's staple services are quite extensive, particularly for home and recreational users. While CompuServe remains the leader in business-oriented information, AOL has been aggressively expanding in this area, adding such services as @times—*The New York Times* online, *Time Magazine* online, *Business Week*, and Cable News Network. Other staples include *Compton's Encyclopedia*, NBC online, *National Geographic*, stock quotations, and even online courses for college credit. AOL maintains an extensive collection of downloadable software and text files as well as a chat feature enabling logged-in users to speak with each other.

America Online's Internet capabilities are developing swiftly. AOL's e-mail system allows users to send and receive messages through the Internet. Users can be reached at **username@aol.com**, so a typical address might be **lkristy@aol.com**.

Users of America Online can also access the more than ten thousand USENET newsgroups found on the Internet (for further discussion, see chapter 9). Groups can be selected either by typing a specific name or by using a hierarchical menu. By maintaining a collection of newsgroups, users can follow and view unread messages at their leisure.

World Wide Web access, using a customized AOL browser, is also available. When you first enter the Web, you are greeted with a topical directory of popular Web sites. This provides a good place to start surfing the Web. Although AOL's Web browser is not as robust as Netscape, it is acceptable for the beginner.

As with its other Internet implementations, America Online has greatly simplified the File Transfer Protocol (FTP) process. Using a menu system, you can choose from a preset group of FTP sites or enter an Internet address to connect to a site not listed. Once you choose the Connect option, AOL will automatically log you in using the anonymous FTP convention (discussed in chapter 11). Navigating through directories and downloading files is simple with AOL's graphical interface. FTP doesn't get much easier than this. Telnet and Gopher capabilities are also available. As with FTP, each offers a list of good starting points but also allows you to venture in your own direction.

Located within AOL's Clubs & Interests section are a number of forums. Among them is the Religion & Ethics Forum, where a variety of Christian information is located. The Religion & Ethics Forum is broken up into several folders including Christianity Doctrine/Theology, Christian Fellowship, and Christian Living. Within each of these folders are a vast number of dynamic discussion topics. Since any user can start a new folder, new topics appear and disappear daily. Similarly, Focus on the Family recently launched a forum on AOL. In addition to discussions, you can read all of Focus's magazines and letters and learn more about this significant ministry.

Within AOL's extensive software library, six categories directly apply to Christians—Christianity Library I, Christianity Library II, Christianity Library III, Christianity Library IV, Homiletics Library, and Bible Study Programs. The four Christianity libraries attest to the large number of files available, ranging from Bible games to publications including the *American Family Association Journal*. America Online also provides an online King James Bible, which can be searched by passage or word.

In late 1994, Christianity Today Incorporated created a special AOL section called Christianity Online. Because of the significant nature of this section, Christianity Online will be specially profiled in the next section.

America Online prohibits profanity and pornography on its network. However, AOL chat sessions have been known to push these limits quite often. Fortunately, AOL has parental controls that allow parents to limit access to certain features, including instant messages and chat sessions. Nevertheless, USENET newsgroups and the World Wide Web expose significant weaknesses in AOL's parental controls. There are a number of pornographic USENET groups that, although they do not appear on AOL's list of groups, are accessible if you know their names. The Web is similar in that AOL doesn't help you find the pornography, but it doesn't restrict it either. Since AOL considers both USENET and the Web external to their service, they don't provide strong parental controls. Be very cautious of this if you have children who use the service.

America Online costs $9.95 per month and includes five hours of online time. AOL's pricing structure is convenient because the base cost includes all services. If you exceed five hours per month, additional time is billed at $2.95 per hour. To join America Online call 1-800-827-6364.

Profile: Christianity Online

In a move similar to the creation of the Christian Interactive Network (CIN), Christianity Today Incorporated (CTi) founded Christianity Online as a service on America Online. The mission of Christianity Online is "To connect Christians around the world through instant electronic communications; to provide access to a wide array of Christian content; and to affirm Christian values within a secular context and culture." Much to their credit, CTi is not limiting Christianity Online to its own publications. It intends to be a broad provider of Christian online resources.

At the heart of Christianity Online lie many electronic magazines including *Christianity Today, Marriage Partnership, Leadership, Campus Life, Christian Woman, Christian History, Christian Computing,* and *The Christian Reader.* Both current and back issues are available for browsing or searching by keyword. The mere presence of so many Christian magazines makes Christianity Online an excellent value. Topical discussion groups and live online discussions are also popular features. In addition, users can reach AOL's other Christian resources (such as the Religion and Ethics Forum and the searchable Bible) through the Christianity Online menu. This menu is shown in figure 3.

Christianity Online has announced major expansion plans including the addition of more magazines, Bible reference libraries, Christian software, ministry job listings, and online shopping. They also hope to include distance learning courses and searchable online directories of Christian colleges and seminaries.

As with other services of America Online, there are no additional costs (above the normal AOL charges) to use Christianity Online. If you are already an AOL member, you can reach Christianity Online by selecting **Goto Keyword** and entering **Christianity**. To subscribe to Christianity

Figure 3

Christianity
Online

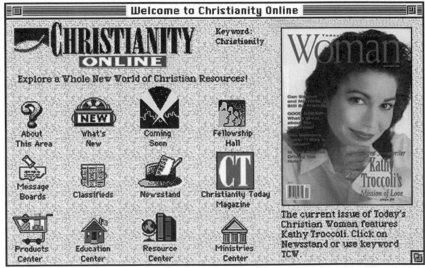

Online/America Online you can either call America Online at 1-800-827-6364 or call *Christianity Today* at 1-800-413-9747, extension 105606.

CompuServe

CompuServe is the oldest of the five services profiled in this book and probably the most expansive. While CompuServe Information Service (CIS) clearly shows its roots as a business-oriented service, there are more than enough resources available for the average family.

At its most basic level, CompuServe uses a text-based interface that is fast and efficient but difficult to manage. To access CompuServe in this text mode you would simply dial in using your terminal emulation software. This is seen below.

```
CompuServe                                                    BASIC

1 Communications
2 News/Weather
3 Sports
4 The Electronic MALL & Shopping
5 Games
6 Entertainment
7 Travel
8 Education
9 Stock Quotes and Personal Finance
10 Magazines
11 Health
12 Member Assistance
13 Access Complete CompuServe Service

Enter choice !
```

You can greatly improve CompuServe navigation by acquiring a product called the CompuServe Information Manager (CIM) from CIS. The CIM is available for the DOS, Windows, and Mac platforms under the names DOSCIM, WinCIM, and MacCIM respectively. These software packages allow you to access CompuServe through a graphical interface that incorporates menus, icons, and even sounds to make the ride friendlier. Figure 4 shows the WinCIM interface; the DOSCIM and MacCIM interfaces look similar.

The explosion of the World Wide Web means that a graphical interface is mandatory to fully enjoy the Internet. Therefore, it is to the user's advantage to acquire the appropriate CIM software for their platform.

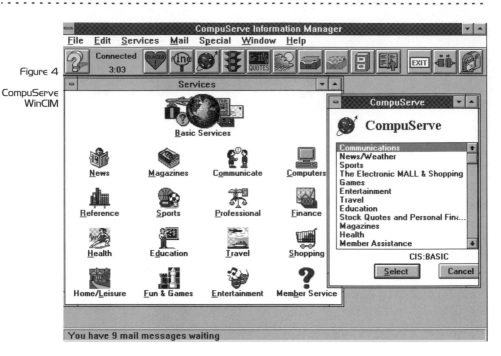

Figure 4

CompuServe
WinCIM

Although CompuServe is not the flashiest of systems, its staple services are fairly extensive. Staples within the realm of CompuServe's Basic services include an electronic mall, *Roger Ebert's Reviews and Features*, *Associated Press Online*, *U.S. News & World Report*, *Peterson's College Database*, and *Zagat Restaurant Guide*. Recently CompuServe changed its pricing structure and added many new services, including Christian ones, within the Basic services pricing. These resources include *Books In Print*, the White House Forum, Legal Forum, Warner Brothers Records, NCAA Collegiate Sports Network, E*TRADE Stock Market Game, and hundreds of vendor forums.

CIS forums are topical discussion groups where you can post messages to public boards or download software programs. If you are interested in broad religious discussion rather than exclusively Christian, you will want to join the Religion Forum.

You can find the Religion Forum by selecting the Home/Leisure icon from the main menu, selecting Special Interest Forums menu, and then choosing the Religion Forum. The quick way to reach the Religion Forum is by typing `Go Religion`. Within the Religion Forum there are topical subgroups including Christianity, Interfaith Dialog, Catholic & Orthodox, Ministry Issues, and Messianic Believers.

Picture the forum structure like a filing room. The Religion Forum is one file cabinet among many. In the Religion cabinet, there are drawers labeled Christianity, Ministry Issues, and so on. Within each of the drawers are folders that hold discussions and other information about a particular facet of the main topic. For instance, within the Christianity drawer you might find one discussion on baptism, another on God's sovereignty, and yet another on Bible software. In fact, the Christianity section contains over a hundred topics of interest. In addition to the discussion topics there are libraries that contain texts, pictures, and software ranging from online magazines to electronic Bibles.

One of CompuServe's Christian forums is an organization called the Christian Interactive Network (CIN). The CIN is much larger than a typical forum; it is actually an online service within an online service. Because of CIN's significance it will be exclusively profiled in the next section.

As a member of CompuServe, your Internet address is **username@com-puserve.com**; however, there is a slight trick to it. All of CompuServe's usernames are actually two numbers separated by a comma. Therefore, a typical CompuServe address would be **74632,3160**. When you send e-mail to **74632,3160** via the Internet, you must replace the comma with a period, so a message would be addressed to **74632.3160@compuserve.com**.

CompuServe allows users to surf the World Wide Web using a built-in browser called Air Mosaic. While not as good as Netscape, it is superior to AOL's browser. USENET newsgroups are also available. CIS allows you to navigate newsgroups using a menu system or directly by typing the name of a particular group. CIS also features Telnet and File Transfer Protocol capability. Don't worry if these terms seem strange; all of them will be addressed in upcoming chapters.

Caution is in order regarding children's use of CompuServe, since it is filled with adult material. From the pornographic USENET groups to digitized photographs from *Playboy*, there is a variety of material that is neither glorifying to God nor edifying to man. Unfortunately, CompuServe does not offer adequate parental restriction capabilities, so parents should keep an eye on their children when using CIS.

Similar to America Online, CompuServe charges $9.95 per month for 5 hours of online time, regardless of connection speed. Additional hours are billed at the rate of $2.95 per hour. Premium services, with varying price structures, are also available. CompuServe can be reached at 1-800-848-8199.

Profile: Christian Interactive Network

Mid-1994 saw a significant advance in Christian implementation of online capabilities with the establishment of the Christian Interactive Network. CIN was founded by Greg Darby as a "Christ-centered ministry dedicated to reaching out into the technology marketplace and providing the Good News of Jesus Christ to a lost 'new' world." Rather than building a stand-alone service, CIN was established as a Premium CompuServe service. As such, the CIN can be reached only through CompuServe by typing **Go CIN**.

In a broad sense, CIN provides an arena for prayer, information, support, education, and the furtherance of the Great Commission. More specifically, CIN is subdivided into six main forums (which function exactly like CompuServe's other forums). Currently the six forums are Ministry Outreach, Publishers Corner, World Missions, Christian Homeschool, World Crisis Network, and Church Connection. CIN also has a Campus Crusade for Christ forum, but it is primarily a private forum for Crusade affiliates. Within these forums are topical discussion groups (up to twenty-four per forum), library sections with a variety of articles and software resources, and conference rooms for private and public discussions.

Figure 5

Christian
Interactive
Network

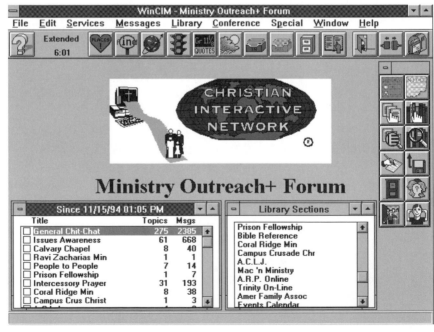

Ministry Outreach is the most frequently visited forum on CIN. In addition to the General Chit-Chat group, topical discussion sections include Prison Fellowship, Campus Crusade for Christ, Probe Ministries, the American Center for Law and Justice, and the American Family Association. Each of the discussion groups has a corresponding library of files that includes information about the ministries, current articles of interest to the Christian community, and a variety of useful ministry resources. Ministry Outreach is currently the only section with established public conference rooms including a Prayer Chapel, Teen Chat, and Fellowship Hall. Conference rooms allow members who are logged on simultaneously to hold conversations with each other. Ministry Outreach, like the other four CIN forums, also allows you to hold one-on-one conversations with other members online in the forum. Figure 5 shows a typical screen from the Christian Interactive Network.

You will find a variety of Christian publishers represented in the Publishers Corner Forum. Members include Logos Research and Parsons Technology (Bible study software developers), *Christian Computing Magazine*, and the Christian Film and Television Commission's *MovieGuide*. In addition to the publishers, there is a Writers Study for experienced and published Christian writers to share stories, tips, and even critique each other's work. The library sections include software demos, press releases, online movie guides, and other reference material.

The World Missions Forum is probably CIN's greatest asset. This forum offers Christians the opportunity to interact with missionary organizations. More importantly, it provides a way for missionaries from all over the world to correspond, share prayer requests, and even raise support from a large and diverse group of believers. Such communication is facilitated by the fact that CompuServe has access numbers in over a hundred countries around the world including the United Kingdom, Europe, Japan, Australia, Chile, Hungary, Israel, South Africa, and South Korea. Some of the mission groups with a presence on the Christian Interactive Network include Youth With A Mission (YWAM), Food for the Hungry, Mission Aviation Fellowship, and International Teams. Within the library sections you can learn more about a particular missionary agency or read about significant events occurring on the mission field. This forum alone could be a key factor in world evangelization in the coming years.

Responding to a growing field, the fourth forum is Christian Homeschool. This forum offers homeschoolers and those interested in homeschooling the opportunity to compare notes, evaluate homeschooling resources, and generally network with one another. The opportunity to regularly interact with numerous homeschoolers is a valuable resource to homeschooling parents. Discussion topics include Just for Kids, Reviews, Time Management, Math/Science, Bible Issues, and Legal and Political Issues. Currently the library sections include Educational Software, Home-school Resources, and *Practical Homeschooling Magazine*. As with the other forums, the library sections offer a variety of useful magazines, software, and references at minimal cost.

Food for the Hungry, a Christian relief and development organization, sponsors the World Crisis Network (WCN) Forum. This forum provides a central location for information about current crises, news briefs, and country profiles. Additional discussion and file topics include service opportunities, articles about giving, opinion pieces, and other information relevant to world issues and feeding the hungry. Although the WCN doesn't generate the magnitude of traffic that other CIN forums do, it addresses critical needs which should concern Christians.

The Church Connection forum provides an electronic meetinghouse for churches and their members. The Church on the Way, Coral Ridge Presbyterian, and Calvary Chapel were the first congregations to join the Church Connection. Despite its limited membership at the present, this forum provides a good arena for members and inquirers alike.

The Christian Interactive Network is a combination of free and fee-based features. Some areas of CIN are available at no additional charge beyond the CompuServe basic rate. Others, such as the homeschooling forums, require an additional fee. If you are already a CompuServe member, type **Go CIN** for the Christian Interactive Network. If you do not have a CIS account, call 1-800-279-LORD (1-800-279-5673) to purchase a membership kit, including the latest version of the CIM software.

Delphi

Delphi is unique among the commercial online services. Its greatest strength lies in the level of Internet access that it offers. If you are looking for a complete, albeit text-based, Internet solution without the difficulty of a UNIX shell or SLIP/PPP connection, then Delphi is your best bet. Unlike the other commercial services, Delphi doesn't require proprietary interface software. Delphi recently released an optional graphical interface, but it differs little from the text-only menus. You will, however, need a terminal emulator to access Delphi. Connecting to the service involves calling a local access number, typing **@D** at the prompt, hitting Return, then entering your username and password. A typical Delphi log on sequence is shown below.

```
CONNECT 14400

@D

TELENET
301 5701G

TERMINAL= (Hit Return)

@c delphi

DELPHI CONNECTED

Username: ECROWN
Password:

Hello ECROWN

Welcome to DELPHI
Copyright (c) 1994
Delphi Internet Services


MAIN Menu:

Business and Finance      Member Directory
Computing Groups          News, Weather, and Sports
Conference                Reference and Education
Custom Forums             Shopping
CLECTROPOLIS (Games)      Travel and Leisure
Entertainment             Using DELPHI
Groups and Clubs          Workspace
Internet Services         HELP
Mail                      EXIT

MAIN>What do you want to do?
```

Although Delphi uses a menu-based approach, there is often more than one way to reach a particular service. For instance, you may access the Internet USENET newsgroups through the Internet Services menu, or from a particular discussion-group menu. Although text-based services are usually more cryptic than graphical ones, Delphi does an admirable job of making resources accessible.

Delphi's method of integrating resources is particularly notable. For instance, to find Christian-oriented Gopher pages, you could go to the Internet Services section, choose Gopher, then search for Christian information. Your other option is to select the Groups and Clubs menu, go to the Theological Network section, and then select Gopher. This approach automatically presents you with a list of theological Gopher pages to explore. Hopefully, this versatility will be emulated by other commercial online services in the future.

Delphi offers a hearty collection of staple services. Some of the staples include online shopping with AutoVantage and Book Stacks Unlimited, UPI Business News, *Donaghue's Money Fund Report*, *Grolier's Encyclopedia*, the Online Gourmet, and a Trivia Tournament.

Of the commercial online services, Delphi is the only one to offer all of the major Internet tools: e-mail, USENET newsgroups, Telnet, FTP, Gopher, and the WWW. These tools all use a custom menu-driven interface. Users on Delphi can be reached at **username@delphi.com**, so a typical address might be **cseager@delphi.com**.

The Theological Network is found within the Groups and Clubs menu. Although not limited to Christianity, there is a fair amount of Christian information available. Areas of interest within the Theological Network include New Testament Studies, Christian Theological Differences, Book Reviews & Reading List, and a Clergy Meetinghouse. Within these and other subgroups you will find topical discussions, online articles, and software packages to download. A quick peek into the New Testament Studies file section reveals such resources as the Latin Vulgate New Testament, a picture of the map of nations from Ezekiel 38, and a comparison of the major Christian creeds. The Theological Network section also contains a sampling of Christian Internet resources. Shown below is a screen shot of the Theological Network section of Delphi.

```
Theological Network Menu:

Announcements          Set Preferences
Conference             Shopping Service
Databases (Files)      Topic Descriptions
Entry Log              Usenet Discussion Groups
Forum (Messages)       Who's Here
Internet Gopher        Workspace
MAIL (Electronic       Help
Member Directory       Exit
Poll

Theology>What do you want to do?
```

Parents need to be very cautious with children who use this service as Delphi does not provide any restrictions or parental controls.

Delphi has two major service plans—the 10/4 and the 20/20. The 10/4 offers four hours of monthly usage for $10.00 with additional hours costing $4.00 each. For more active users, the 20/20 offers twenty hours for $20.00 per month, with a $1.00 charge per additional hour. If you want full Internet access with either plan, a $3.00 monthly fee is incurred. In addition, if you access Delphi through a dial-up number (as opposed to reaching Delphi via Internet Telnet) there are further charges during the 6:00 A.M. to 6:00 P.M. weekday peak period that apply to both the 10/4 and 20/20 plans. The peak time charge is a steep $9.00 per hour, so it is best to use Delphi during evenings and weekends. You can reach Delphi at 1-800-695-4005. Despite Delphi's recent acquisition by MCI, it has not kept up with the Internet explosion during the past year and so cannot be recommended.

Prodigy

Prodigy, a joint venture of IBM and Sears, was designed from the ground up as an easy to use family-oriented service. Unlike some systems, there is no text-only interface—all interfaces are graphical and all have the same look and feel to them. The interface is rather intuitive, except that it relies more on menu selections than icons for common actions. Once you become acclimated to the Prodigy interface, navigating becomes simple. Figure 6 shows the Prodigy opening screen.

The biggest difference between Prodigy and the other services is its use of advertisements. As you move around Prodigy, different ads appear at the bottom of your screen. By selecting an ad you can learn more about the vendor or product featured. Prodigy states that the ads help them to keep prices low. Much like with television commercials, they slow down the whole process and can be quite annoying.

Prodigy's staple services are quite good if you are looking for family and educational materials. Its repertoire of references includes *Grolier's Academic American Encyclopedia*, *Consumer Reports*, and *Magill's Survey of Cinema*. There are travel guides for over a dozen major cities as well as regional travel guides and trip planning helps. Prodigy also has sound clips to supplement certain digitized photos, graphics, and online articles. If your computer system has a sound card, you can listen to daily business news, sports updates, and other noteworthy sound bites. With features ranging from a Sesame Street section to college guides and discussions, it

Figure 6

Prodigy
Opening
Screen

is no surprise that Prodigy has more children and young adults online than any other major service.

Prodigy offers several options that make online access easy for the whole family. It is possible, for example, to set up additional accounts for family members as derivatives of your main account, with no additional charge. Furthermore, as the master account holder you can restrict sections of Prodigy that those dependent accounts can access. This is particularly helpful if you don't want your seven-year-old to access discussion groups of R-rated movies or to explore the many questionable USENET groups. Prodigy prohibits any offensive, pornographic, or adult material online. They review all messages that are posted to Prodigy discussion groups and reject any that contain unacceptable material. This screening is not extended to private e-mail messages or USENET groups, however. While some of their policies are controversial, Prodigy is definitely the most child-protective of the services profiled here.

In comparison to other online services, Prodigy's Christian resources are on the thin side. Most Christian material is located in the Prodigy bulletin boards (BBs). Found within the Communications section, Prodigy has over a thousand BBs, which are the online discussion groups. Within a BB, members can select a topic, read messages, and post responses. The three bulletin boards with the most Christian-related material are Religion Concourse 1, Religion Concourse 2, and Music.

While the Religion Concourse 1 BB is not exclusively Christian, there are a large number of Christian subgroups there. These include Catholic, Bible, Presbyterian, Pentecostal, Lutheran, and others. Non-Christian groups such as the Jehovah's Witnesses are also present. These areas are good for sharing information, asking questions, and pursuing general discussions with others. However, these groups are *not* for proselytizing or attacking other denominations or faiths. Both of these activities are expressly prohibited on these boards, and you will be reprimanded if you disobey the rules. There *is* plenty of room for discussion within these electronic town halls; just be aware of the rules before posting anything. Figure 7 shows the Religion Concourse 1 BB. Notice the ad shown at the bottom of the screen.

The Religion Concourse 2 BB topics include Church/State, Cults/Opinion/Info, and Prayer Line. Other religious groups, such as Wicca, also have subjects on this BB. A monthly debate highlights Religion Concourse 2. Within the Music BB are the Contemporary Christian Music (CCM) and Religious Music categories. These areas provide excellent opportunities to debate and discuss the Christian music scene.

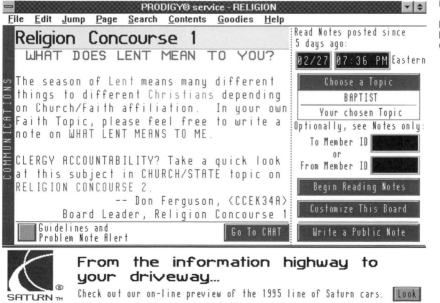

Figure 7

Prodigy
Religion
Concourse I

Downloading software in Prodigy is more restrictive than in the other services. Most of the available software is organized by distributor rather than by subject. There are often additional charges associated with downloads. This is one of Prodigy's major weaknesses as a commercial online service.

Prodigy was the first commercial service to offer a graphical World Wide Web browser (see chapter 13), which has become one of its most popular features. This gives Prodigy users access to the hottest Internet service without the hassle of a SLIP/PPP connection. Additional Internet services include e-mail, USENET discussion groups, and the Internet BB for discussion of topics related to the Internet. Other people on the Internet may send mail to your Prodigy account by addressing messages to **username@prodigy.com**. Thus the Internet address **xrwy93a@prodigy.com** corresponds to a Prodigy user whose account name is **XRWY93A**. As you can see from the example, the address is not case sensitive.

Prodigy's pricing remains competitive with other services. The basic plan costs $9.95 per month for five hours of Prodigy use, including spending time on the World Wide Web. Online time beyond five hours is then billed at $2.95 per hour. The 30/30 Plan costs $29.95 per month and features 30 hours of online time, again including all of the Prodigy services. Additional hours beyond the base 30 will cost $2.95 per hour. You can reach Prodigy at 1-800-PRODIGY (1-800-776-3449).

Christian Online Services

Didax

Under development for a few years, Didax has been designed from the ground up as a unique Christian service. Rather than simply providing a place for individual users to come together, Didax seeks to build the electronic infrastructure to link Christian organizations, missions agencies, churches, and families together.

Attempting to become the state of the art Christian online service, Didax has chosen to build their system around the Lotus Notes software product. Notes runs on all the major computer platforms and allows users to create private forums, work efficiently with information databases, set up e-mail accounts for everyone in an organization or family, and even work offline to reduce costs. Such capabilities mean that an organization could use Didax as an internal networking system, and individual users could dial into the service from home. Such a configuration will also foster two-way communication between Christians and various ministry organizations.

From the resource standpoint, Didax plans to offer the same core services found on the other commercial systems. However, the pornographic and offensive material often found on other online systems will not be permitted. When the system is complete, Didax should provide a comprehensive resource center for individuals and organizations to access.

To receive further details about Didax or to be placed on their mailing list, call 1-800-935-3263. You can also contact their main office at 1-703-391-6050.

OnePlace

Another Christian online service currently under development is One-Place: A Christian Village. OnePlace is unique in that the entire system is being designed with Internet access in mind. Unlike the other commercial online services, which have scrambled to adapt to the exponential growth of the Internet, OnePlace is attempting to take advantage of the Internet's momentum by building its system around the current Internet tools.

Like the commercial online services, OnePlace plans to offer national news, travel services, banking and financial information, downloadable software, e-mail, and similar staple features. Additionally, OnePlace will provide full access to the vast array of Christian resources found on the Internet, including mailing lists, USENET groups, Gopher servers, and World Wide Web pages. Christian software demos and products will also be available.

OnePlace will use a SLIP/PPP connection to employ a modified version of the World Wide Web browser Mosaic (discussed in chapter 13). This will give users a multimedia interface to the Internet. Subscribers may also access OnePlace using standard terminal emulation software.

Announced pricing for the service starts at $9.95 per month for four hours of use or $21.95 for ten hours. Additional hours will be billed at $3.00 per hour. For more information about OnePlace: A Christian Village, you can call 1-713-929-1577 or send e-mail to **oneplace@vax1.village.com**.

5

Internet Connections

While commercial online services are the most popular choice for new explorers in cyberspace, many experienced users prefer a more in-depth Internet connection. For those who are less concerned about ease of use and more interested in a greater breadth of Internet services, there are three major choices—UNIX shell accounts, SLIP or PPP connections, and proprietary Internet interfaces.

Definitions

Before your eyes glaze over at the mention of UNIX, TCP/IP, SLIP, and PPP, a few definitions are in order. UNIX, pronounced "you-nicks," is the name of a computer operating system originally developed over twenty-five years ago by Bell Laboratories. Since then it has undergone many advances and now appears in numerous incarnations marketed by different vendors. While it is difficult to believe that a computer operating system could last so long in such a rapidly changing technological environment, its longevity is a testimony to the versatility and power of UNIX. Unfortunately, UNIX remains a rather cryptic text-based system employing obscure commands such as **ls** and **cd**.

TCP/IP stands for Transmission Control Protocol/Internet Protocol. More will be said about this in chapter 7, but suffice it to say that TCP/IP is a suite of protocols that dictate how all of the computers connected to the Internet communicate with each other. SLIP and PPP are two standards that allow computers to communicate to each other using TCP/IP over a dial-up line. The good news is that like telephones, televisions, and other modern technologies, you don't have to understand how everything works under the hood in order to benefit.

UNIX Shell Accounts

Since the majority of computers connected to the Internet use the UNIX operating system, it is logical that most Internet services are UNIX-based. Therefore, one way to gain access to the majority of Internet services is to obtain a UNIX shell account. A *shell* is the name given to an interface that you interact with. The interface actually accepts your commands, interprets them, then passes them on to the UNIX host—hence, the term UNIX shell. Unlike the commercial online services, you cannot call up the UNIX Company and request an account, because no such company exists. Rather, you need to contact an Internet service provider who offers UNIX shell accounts.

Finding a Provider

Finding providers is often like solving a puzzle. You see, the easiest way to find an Internet provider is to look on the Internet. Obviously you can't get on the Internet until you find a provider, hence the quandary. Below is a table of some nationwide Internet providers that can help you start:

Provider Name	Phone Number	E-Mail Address
Advantis	800-888-4103	info@advantis.com
HoloNet	510-704-0160	info@holonet.net
JvNCnet	609-897-7300	info@jvnc.net
The Pipeline	212-267-3636	info@pipeline.com
PSINet	800-827-7482	info@psi.com
Netcom	800-353-6600	info@netcom.com
NovaLink	800-274-2814	info@novalink.com
UUNET	800-488-6385	info@uunet.uu.net

If you choose to get a UNIX shell account or SLIP/PPP account, you can begin by obtaining an account with one of these providers. First call and find out if they have an access number that is a local call for you. Once you are online, check out the USENET groups `alt.internet.access.wanted` and `alt.internet.services` for postings about finding providers. You can also browse a list of Internet providers organized by area code on the World Wide Web. The list, sponsored by Network-USA, is located at Uniform Resource Locator (URL): `http://www.netusa.net/ISP/`. Finally, there is a Public Dialup Internet Access List (PDIAL) available via e-mail. Just send a note to `info-deli-server@netcom.com` with a subject line (not message text) that reads `send pdial`.

Because costs can vary greatly, it is worth doing some research before signing up with a service provider. In fact, there may even be a free UNIX service offered by a local library or organization. Next to cost, the biggest factor to consider is support. Since UNIX can be a mysterious and confusing operating system, helpful service representatives can make all the difference. Again, if you are unsure where to begin, sign up with one of the providers listed here and then research other options. When you find a better, easier, or cheaper provider, simply switch.

While some UNIX providers offer customized software to make the log-in process more user-friendly, most do not. Hence you need to have a terminal emulation software package on your computer. Such communication software was described in greater depth in chapter 3. Most modems come with this software, and both Microsoft Windows and OS/2 include minimal terminal emulation applications.

Making the Connection

The general procedure for connecting to a UNIX shell account is to first configure your modem and terminal emulation through your communications software. Every communications software package has its own configuration procedure. Your best bet is to check the instructions that came with your modem and communications software to learn how to configure them properly. If you lack documentation, check the help menu on your communications software or look for choices like "setup," "communications," "configuration," or "line settings." A typical configuration screen is shown in figure 8.

Once you have located the communications parameters, you will need to configure the appropriate bps rate, number of bits, parity, stop bits, and terminal emulation as specified by your Internet provider. These parameters simply ensure that your computer is speaking the same dialect as the computer you are calling. A typical configuration might be 14,400 bps, 8 bits, no parity, one stop bit, using VT100 emulation. Once you are configured properly, you are ready to dial your Internet provider.

From your communications software, dial the appropriate number and wait until your modem connects with the distant end. At this point

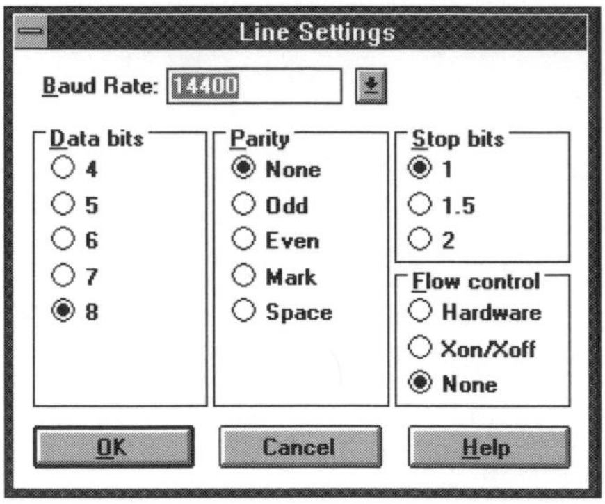

Figure 8

Line Settings

```
┌──────────────────────────────────────────────┐
│ ▬          Line Settings                       │
├──────────────────────────────────────────────┤
│  Baud Rate: [14400]          ▼                 │
│  ┌Data bits┐ ┌Parity────┐ ┌Stop bits┐         │
│  │ ○ 4     │ │ ◉ None   │ │ ◉ 1     │         │
│  │ ○ 5     │ │ ○ Odd    │ │ ○ 1.5   │         │
│  │ ○ 6     │ │ ○ Even   │ │ ○ 2     │         │
│  │ ○ 7     │ │ ○ Mark   │ ┌Flow control┐      │
│  │ ◉ 8     │ │ ○ Space  │ │ ○ Hardware │      │
│  │         │ │          │ │ ○ Xon/Xoff │      │
│  │         │ │          │ │ ◉ None     │      │
│  └─────────┘ └──────────┘ └────────────┘      │
│  [   OK   ]  [  Cancel  ]  [   Help   ]        │
└──────────────────────────────────────────────┘
```

you may need to hit the Return key a few times in order to get a prompt. Typically, you will receive a prompt that says Username, User or some variation of this theme. If this is your first call, you may see something like:

```
Type new if you are a new user
```

Just follow the online instructions to set up your account. Otherwise, enter your username and hit Return. Be aware that UNIX is case sensitive so **Rshearer** is different from **rshearer**. Next, you will be prompted to enter your password. After you correctly enter your password and hit Return, you will see either a menu or a UNIX shell prompt. The following example shows how to set up an account online with a typical Internet provider.

```
Online Communications Service
Don't have an account? Login as new (no password).

username: new
Password:

Welcome to Online Communications. Please enter your selection:

1: Online Communications Account Setup (Credit card users only)

2: Display Local Dialup Access Numbers and Pricing Info

3: Send us your postal mail address, we'll mail an account application to you.

4 or Control-C: Hangup

Enter selection (1-10): 1

In order to set up your account online we will need a username of your choice(1-
10 characters long, all lower case), a password (at least 6 characters long and
```

```
includes at least one number), your real name, address, and telephone number,
and your credit card number and expiration date.

Do you want to fill out an online application? (y/n) y

Desired user name: christian
Checking user name for availability, please wait.
Username christian is o.k.
Enter password: john316
Enter desired full name visible to others: Chris Christian
Enter your real name: Chris Christian
Enter your street address: 17 Church Lane
Enter apartment or suite number, etc.:
Enter city: Baltimore
Enter state or province and country: MD
Enter zip or postal code: 21287

. . . (Enter credit card information for billing)

The following account has been activated:
username: christian
password: john316

When you log in, be sure to read the online help by typing help.

Enjoy surfing the Internet with Online Communications!
```

The examples that follow show typical opening screens of UNIX shell accounts. The first is an example of a menu-based UNIX shell. The second is the more common UNIX interface, which consists of some opening comments followed by a generic prompt. Take note that the password is not displayed when you enter it (for security reasons). Your provider's service may look different from these examples, but they'll give you an idea of what to expect.

UNIX Shell Account with Menu

```
Online Communications Service
Don't have an account? Login as new (no password).

username: christian
Password:

Last login: Sat Apr 15 09:48:15 from annex1.online.net

    CHOOSE TERMINAL TYPE
```

```
                    1. Vt 100 (vt100)
                    2. ANSI (ansi)
                    3. Enter preferred terminal type

        Pick your selection number? 1

        You have selected a DEC Vt 100 Terminal

    Welcome to Online Communications!

        o Send Email to "help" for customer support.
          Send Email to "office" for billing inquiries.

    Checking for any new mail . . .

                              Main Menu

    1 Communications: Personal mail, network news, etc.

    2 Internet Services: FTP, Gopher, Telnet, Lynx, etc.

    3 Files: Copy, delete, edit, upload/download files

    4 Configure Defaults: Configure default mailer, news reader, etc..

    5 Help and Information: Help for using the system, on-line books of interest,
    and more.

    6 Send Feedback to System Operator
    _____


    Select choice [or top, exit, logoff]:
```

UNIX Shell Account with Prompt

```
Online Communications Service
Don't have an account? Login as new (no password).

username: christian
Password:

Last login: Sat Apr 15 09:55:23 from annex1.online.net

    CHOOSE TERMINAL TYPE

            1. Vt 100 (vt100)
            2. ANSI (ansi)
            3. Enter preferred terminal type

    Pick your selection number? 1
```

```
        You have selected a DEC Vt 100 Terminal

Welcome to Online Communications!

    o Send Email to "help" for customer support.
      Send Email to "office" for billing inquiries.

Checking for any new mail . . .

online:[users/christian]
```

Although the specifics vary among UNIX providers, all of the major Internet services (including e-mail, USENET newsgroups, FTP, Telnet, Gopher, and the WWW) should be available to you. Additional information about each of these services can be found in each of their respective chapters later in this book.

Essential UNIX Commands

Some fundamental UNIX commands are needed to navigate your shell account. Be aware that because of different UNIX configurations, not every command will necessarily work on every system. Check with your provider to see if they have online or hard copy documentation listing additional UNIX commands appropriate to their system. Note that italicized words are parameters which must be replaced when issuing a command.

Command	*Function*
cat *filename*	Displays the contents of text file called *filename*
cd *name*	Changes to the directory *name*, which must be a subdirectory of the current directory
cd */name1/name2*	Changes to the directory */name1/name2*
cd ..	Backs up one directory level
cd /	Backs up to the top-level directory
dir	Lists files in the current directory
elm	Runs Elm, a user-friendly mailing system
exit	Logs off of the system
finger	Provides information about *user@domainname* using the *username@domainname* Finger feature
ftp *address*	Opens an FTP connection to the computer at *address*
gopher *address*	Runs Gopher, opening your default Gopher server unless you specify an alternate *address*. The command is typically issued by typing **gopher**
logoff or logout	Logs off of the system

`ls`	Lists files in the current directory
`ls -1`	Lists files and their sizes (in bytes)
`|more`	Pauses a listing at the end of every screen rather than scrolling continuously. Used in conjunction with other commands such as `ls` and `cat`. For example, `ls |more` will list files pausing the list after every screen. To continue, press the space bar
`lynx`	Launches Lynx, a text-based World Wide Web browser
`man command`	Displays manual information about a particular *command*
`mkdir name`	Makes a new directory called *name*
`rm filename`	Removes (deletes) the file called *filename*
`mail`	Runs Mail, the default UNIX mailing system
`pine`	Runs Pine, a user-friendly mailing system
`quit`	Terminates an FTP connection
`telnet address`	Establishes a Telnet connection to the computer at *address*
`tin`	Invokes Tins, a user-friendly threaded newsreader to read USENET news
`trn`	Invokes Trn, a threaded newsreader to read USENET news
`whois organization`	Looks up *organization* in the Network Information Center (NIC) list of Internet hosts. It will return the domain name information for *organization*

SLIP or PPP Connections

For those who are really ambitious, or consider themselves "Internet power users," a SLIP or PPP account may be the Internet connection of choice. While SLIP and PPP accomplish the same purpose, PPP is the newer and better of the two protocols. Nevertheless, since they are so similar, many Internet providers refer to their service generically as a SLIP/PPP connection.

Necessary Software

Although a SLIP or PPP connection doesn't require any additional hardware, you will need some specialized software, namely a TCP/IP stack. As mentioned earlier, SLIP and PPP are protocols that work with the TCP/IP protocols. Since TCP/IP is not yet a standard product on most home computers, you will probably need to acquire it in order to make a SLIP or PPP connection. Although the easiest way to get the necessary software is to purchase it from the provider of your SLIP/PPP service, you can also obtain TCP/IP software by buying it directly from a manufacturer, downloading it from a commercial online service, or downloading it from the Internet via an anonymous FTP server. The table below lists five anonymous FTP sites that freely allow you to download TCP/IP software. Details about how to use the FTP service are found in chapter 11.

Name	*Platform*	*FTP Address*	*Directory*

MacTCP	Apple Mac	`ftp.austin.apple.com`	`/Apple.Support.Area/`
			`Apple.SW.Upgrades/`
			`Net.and.Comm.SW/`

MacTCP	Apple Mac	`wuarchive.wustl.edu`	`/systems/mac/macintosh/` `comm/`
Trumpet Winsock	IBM/Windows	`wuarchive.wustl.edu`	`/systems/msdos.win3/` `winsock/`
Trumpet Winsock	IBM/Windows	`ftp.ncsa.uiuc.edu`	`/PC/Windows/Mosaic/` `sockets/`
Chameleon Sampler	IBM/Windows	`ftp.netmanage.com`	`/pub/demos/sampler/`

Fortunately, newer operating system releases such as Microsoft Windows 95, Apple System 7.5, and IBM OS/2 3.0 bundle the base TCP/IP in their packages. This development makes SLIP/PPP access significantly easier for the beginner since acquiring the TCP/IP software can be a hassle. Software vendors are hoping to further simplify the process by allowing a one-step setup. Ideally, you will just click on an Internet icon, and the software will perform the necessary configurations and place the call for you. It remains to be seen if this attempt will be successful. Until then you'll have to manipulate the TCP/IP configuration yourself.

Configuration

As with a UNIX shell account, you'll have to configure your communications software with the bps rate, number of bits, parity, and stop bits specified by your provider. In addition, you'll need to configure your TCP/IP software. Typically the TCP/IP software has a selection labeled "setup" or "configuration" that you choose in order to change the communication parameters. You will need to know your Internet Protocol (IP) address, name server address, time server address, and MTU value. These parameters will be given to you by your SLIP/PPP service provider. A typical configuration screen is shown in figure 9.

The relative complexity of setting up a SLIP or PPP account is why you should choose a provider with extensive technical support assistance. Once your system is properly configured, you are ready to make a SLIP/PPP connection. Below is an example of a SLIP log-on session. (The **atdt** command is a Hayes modem command used to dial the phone.)

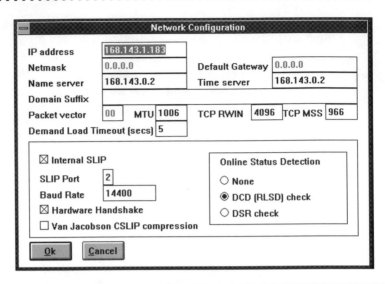

Figure 9

TCP/IP
Configuration

```
SLIP ENABLED
Internal SLIP driver COM2 Baud rate = 14400 Hardware handshaking
My ip = 168.143.1.183 netmask = 0.0.0.0 gateway = 0.0.0.0
Manually dialing.
AFTER LOGGING IN, TYPE THE <ESC> KEY TO RETURN TO NORMAL SLIP
PROCESSING.
SLIP DISABLED
atdt 995-0271
CONNECT 14400

Online Communications Service
Don't have an account? Login as new (no password).

username: christian
Password:

Last login: Mon Apr 17 11:21:20 from annex1.online.net

Online Communications Menu

1) Enter UNIX System
2) SLIP (SLIP users only)
3) PPP (PPP users only)
4) Exit

Enter Number (1-8): 2

Switching to SLIP.
System address is 168.143.0.4. Your address is 168.143.1.183.
<ESC>
SLIP ENABLED
```

Unfortunately, the base TCP/IP software only gives you the ability to make a SLIP/PPP connection. In order to do anything once you are connected, additional software is necessary. There are a number of programs that will enable you to use Internet services such as e-mail, USENET newsgroups, FTP, Telnet, Gopher, and the WWW. Unlike the traditional UNIX shell, you are not limited to text-based implementations of these services. Many easy-to-use graphical programs exist for these Internet tasks. You will find some of these programs at the same anonymous FTP sites listed in the previous chart.

SLIP/PPP Advantages

A SLIP or PPP connection will allow you to use Netscape. Netscape is a multimedia graphical interface which simplifies and enhances the base Internet services such as FTP, Gopher, and the WWW. Essentially it makes Internet surfing more like reading a magazine than playing with a computer. Netscape will be discussed in more detail in chapter 13, but its power and user-friendliness make it a clear advantage of having a SLIP/PPP account. Figure 10 shows a Library of Congress Dead Sea Scrolls exhibit page viewed with a Netscape-style interface.

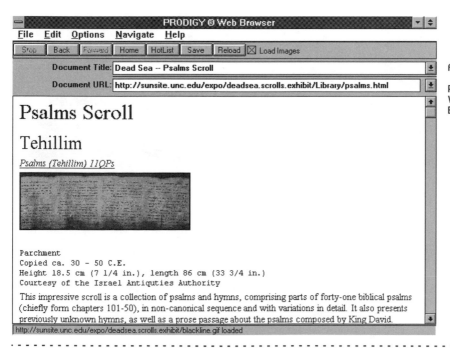

Figure 10

Prodigy Web Browser

Another advantage of a SLIP/PPP connection is that it allows your computer to become a fully functional host on the Internet. As such, you have your own Internet IP address, your own hostname, and can do things like directly download files onto your system via FTP. SLIP and PPP connections can also do multiple tasks at the same time. Suppose you want to download a file while simultaneously checking a USENET group. Assuming you have a fast modem and a powerful system, both will work great. (Without these, your computer may slow to a crawl when attempting multiple Internet tasks.)

Proprietary Internet Interfaces

Recently, a number of Internet providers have developed proprietary Internet interfaces that bridge the gap between inexpensive UNIX shell accounts and powerful SLIP/PPP connections. Led by the Pipeline, an Internet provider based in New York, many online companies have developed proprietary graphical software that allows you to access the Internet as if you had a SLIP or PPP connection. Such software offers a graphical front-end to e-mail, USENET news, Gopher, the WWW, and other Internet services. Figure 11 shows a picture of the Pipeline software.

Figure 11

The
Pipeline

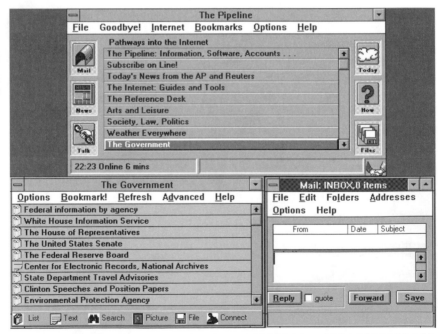

Although you don't gain the multitasking or addressing advantages of a SLIP/PPP account, you can browse the World Wide Web graphically with a Netscape-like interface. Best of all, proprietary Internet connections don't require you to configure a TCP/IP stack before accessing the Internet. Considering that TCP/IP configuration is often the most difficult aspect of a SLIP/PPP connection, many have hailed proprietary Internet software as a breakthrough.

Despite the many advantages of proprietary Internet software, there are two obstacles to its widespread acceptance. Unlike UNIX shell accounts or SLIP/PPP connections, the custom software is not based on a standard but rather has been developed as a proprietary package. Therefore, if Internet providers want to use the software, they must license it from the developers or develop their own products, both of which are cost-prohibitive options. The second obstacle is that TCP/IP software is becoming a standard feature in operating systems. As this occurs, SLIP and PPP account configuration will simplify greatly. Unless proprietary software propagates quickly, it may be overtaken by SLIP/PPP.

Check with your proposed Internet provider to see if they offer any proprietary software to make your Internet journey smoother. Two nationwide Internet providers are PSI and Netcom. PSI bought the Pipeline software shown in figure 11 and have thus made it available to users outside the New York area. Netcom offers an interface called NetCruiser, which, like Pipeline, gives the Internet user a friendly interface for e-mail, FTP, WWW, and the other Internet services. The rapid growth of the Internet, and corresponding delays in companies making their operating systems Internet-ready, have contributed to the growing popularity of these interfaces. Regardless of the future of proprietary Internet software, it is an option worth examining.

6

Christian Bulletin Board Systems

With the explosive growth of the Internet during the last few years, it is easy to forget that there are other online services available. One such service is the computer bulletin board system, also known as a BBS. BBSs are to the Internet what country roads are to superhighways. They aren't as large or flashy, but you might discover an exciting ride. Given that there are over twenty thousand bulletin board systems across the United States, this type of online service is too vast to be overlooked.

What Is a BBS?

Bulletin board systems are a product of the personal computer explosion, which began about fifteen years ago. Not content with isolated computers that sat in dens and basements, some people decided that there would be much to gain if users could come together in an electronic meetinghouse to exchange information and computer resources. Back in those days, the Internet was not as accessible as it is today. There were few commercial online services, and those that did exist were intended for business and professional use. A number of pioneering, and generally altruistic, computer gurus began to write or acquire special software that, with a modem, would allow others to call in to access files or leave messages. Unlike the multiuser chat functions and real-time games found on some commercial systems today, these early online attempts just allowed messages to be posted for others to read later. They functioned much like electronic bulletin boards, hence the name *bulletin board system.*

Over the years much has changed with BBSs. Some are more powerful and easier to use than their commercial counterparts, while others remain cryptic and sparse in their features. Most BBSs are run by a system operator, or Sysop, as a free service to other cyberspace users. There are thousands of resources found on computer BBSs including reference material, software programs, and discussion groups. Some BBSs are focused on specific topics or interests, while others are generic and provide a large diversity of information. Shown below is a menu from a Christian BBS menu.

```
                    CHRISTIAN BBS MAIN MENU
                    ~~~~~~~~~~~~~~~~~~~~~~~~~~

To select a new menu, type in the beginning letter of
that selection (example: type in D for Discussion Groups)

     <D>ISCUSSION GROUPS
     <F>ILE SECTIONS
     <B>ULLETINS
     <U>SER LIST
     <Y>ELL FOR SYSOP

     <1>MAIN MENU    <2>PREV MENU    <3>EMAIL    <4>USER INFO    <5>LOGOFF

Command: D
```

You are probably wondering why anyone would want to leave messages on a computer that isn't on a central network like the Internet. Actually, Sysops have developed a rather creative way of passing information between BBSs so they can behave as if they were truly networked. Since most BBSs run on shoestring budgets, the Sysops cannot afford direct lines to the Internet. Instead, Sysops will configure their systems to automatically dial other BBS computers during the early morning hours and exchange the new information (messages, files, etc.) that they have received. The computers act like organizational phone chains—one system calls another, the two systems exchange their latest information, then they hang up and each call other computers. This continues until all of the computers in a particular phone tree have been updated for the new day. Just as it can take a few hours for a request to be passed down a small group prayer chain, it may take a few days for a message to travel from an East Coast BBS to one on the West Coast. This method may not be fancy, but it is both effective and cheap.

Christian bulletin board systems are exactly what their name suggests—BBSs expressly developed to serve the Christian community. Some are sponsored by churches, while others are individually operated. Christian BBS Sysops have formed loose coalitions with each other using the phone tree concept just explained. These coalitions, often called networks, have been developed to allow nationwide discussion groups and software distribution. Some of the more popular coalitions include the Christian Distribution Network and FamilyNet.

Finding a BBS

One of the more challenging aspects of bulletin board systems is finding them. Those shoestring budgets mentioned earlier mean that you won't find many Christian BBSs advertising in magazines or phone books. To make your search easier, you will find a starter list of Christian bulletin board systems in appendix B. The list is by no means complete, but many area codes are represented. If you cannot find one in the appendix that is local to you, a brief long-distance call may be necessary. Once you have logged on to the BBS, you will likely find an option to examine or download a listing of other Christian BBSs. Using this resource, you should be able to locate one that is within your local calling area. If you cannot find such a list online, leave a message for the Sysop requesting local Christian BBS numbers. Most Sysops are very willing to assist cyberspace travelers. If there are no Christian BBSs in your area, the Sysop may point you to a good non-Christian BBS. Often you will find Christian or Bible-related files and discussion groups on generic BBSs.

A word to the wise: Be suspicious of any local BBS that requests credit card information about you. While it is safe to give such information out to America Online or CompuServe, you probably don't want to relinquish it to an obscure BBS.

Accessing a BBS

Like Delphi and UNIX shells, most BBSs do not require special software to access their systems. You will, however, need your trusty terminal emulation software setup to call the BBS. Most BBSs use communication settings of eight bits, no parity, and one stop bit. Since different BBSs operate at different speeds, it's best to set your software to the highest setting your modem can support. The modems will automatically connect at the highest speed common to both systems. One additional comment concerns busy signals. Most bulletin board systems only have one modem (compared to commercial online services, which have hundreds); therefore, don't be surprised if you get a busy signal. Patience and persistence are required, but keep trying because the payoff is well worth the effort.

If you are a first-time user of a BBS you will probably be told to enter new as your username. At this point the system will probably request further information such as your real name, address, and phone number. This is akin to the initial log-on process for a commercial online service. Once the Sysop validates your information, you will be given free reign to access the BBS.

What Resources Are on BBSs?

Christian bulletin board features vary greatly depending on the particular BBS. One may have various Bibles that you can search online, while another may specialize in evangelism and apologetics. Despite the variety of options, virtually all Christian BBSs contain two core features: topical discussion groups and file sections.

Discussion groups, arranged by topic, may be specific to a bulletin board or may be shared with other systems belonging to the same BBS network. Typical topics include theology, eschatology, Bible software discussion, prayer requests, singles discussion, parenting advice, music and worship, politics, current events, and the like. As you can see, discussion topics can be extensive and diverse. If there is not a discussion group about a particular topic of interest to you, feel free to inform the Sysop. Often the Sysop will carry discussion groups based on the demand of the BBS users; therefore, your request might prompt the addition (or creation) of that particular topical group.

Because any BBS member can upload files to be shared with others, file sections are often more populated than the discussion groups. These files will range from recent articles of interest to the Christian community to games that help you memorize Scripture. Bible timelines, Scripture studies, and book reviews also populate many BBSs. Shown below is a sample file listing with descriptions, just to give you a taste:

```
Files: ['*'=new, <enter>=all, or type a partial filename]:

GODSLOVE.ZIP   110336  12-06-92  The ABC's of Salvation
NEWS1205.SDN    51689  12-11-92  Christian-based newspaper
WISDOM.ZIP     548299  12-16-92  Wisdom of the ages
GODSLUV2.ZIP   110770  12-16-92  A program for your salvation
LOSE.ZIP        18848  12-28-92  "Can You Lose Your Salvation?"
BIBLEV3.ZIP     60412  01-09-93  Verse of the day for your computer
```

```
DEITY.ZIP        16426 01-10-93  A defense of the deity of Christ
ATONE.ZIP         9759 12-16-91  Atonement(Calvinism & Arminianism)
JES_YHWH.ZIP      7188 02-19-91  Is Jesus "Yahweh" (Jehovah)?
HIST_REF.ZIP    101958 01-01-80  History of the Reformation
PRE-EX.ZIP       15318 03-11-91  Pre-existence of Christ
PROTOS.ZIP        7714 02-19-91  "PROTOTOKOS" Meaning & Usage
ABORT-01.ZIP     56875 05-15-92  Menu driven text file on abortion.
BIBLESUM.ZIP      6457 03-14-93  Summary of the Bible by CS Lewis.
NEWTSTEV.ZIP      8816 03-14-93  Historicity of the New Testament.
RUCKMAN.ZIP       4015 03-14-93  Ruckman controversy regarding KJV
IND493.ARJ       11511 04-24-93  Israel News Digest—April 1993
CRI_JW.ZIP        3976 03-28-93  Testimony of ex-Jehovah's Witness
CRI_NOST.ZIP      3063 03-28-93  Newsletter article on Nostradamus
BYCT0593.ZIP      6552 05-13-93  Christian Action Fact Sheet
LETTER.TXT       17846 06-09-93  Open letter from former JW
SECURITY.TXT     96384 05-29-93  Lose your salvation?
HELL.TXT         12928 06-03-93  Is there a literal Hell fire?
HINN-01.TXT       7424 06-03-93  Benny Hinn on Holy Spirit on TBN
ICR-001.TXT      11264 06-03-93  Institute for Creation Research
HR-EMAIL.SDN      5773 04-12-94  Address List of US Congressmen
MOONGOD.COM       9477 04-16-94  ISLAM: Religion of the Moon God.
WESTMNST.ARJ     29703 03-21-93  Westminster Confession of Faith
ORIGIN.ZIP      124615 07-17-94  "How To Teach The Original Greek"
```

Chapter 11 will explore the details of a file transfer; nevertheless, a few brief statements should be made here. The majority of files on BBSs are compressed using some proprietary compression algorithm. Files are compressed so they take less space on the Sysop's computer and take less time to transfer via modem. This means a decompression utility will be necessary. Different BBSs and networks employ different compression techniques so you may need to do some research to determine which software will work. A table of anonymous FTP sites from which decompression programs can be downloaded is given in chapter 11. If you remain uncertain about how to decompress a particular file, send a note to the Sysop and ask. Most Sysops will gladly assist you if you need help. Just remember that they are probably running the system in their spare time, so your patience will be appreciated.

The next two sections are special profiles of resources offered through Christian bulletin boards: the Online Bible and the On-Line Bible College. The Online Bible is a software program distributed and supported through Christian BBSs. The On-Line Bible College (not related to the Online Bible) is a Bible college that offers distance learning using a Christian BBS as its main campus. Both are excellent examples of how cyberspace can be harnessed for the building up of the body of Christ.

Profile: The Online Bible

Larry Pierce started working on the Online Bible in 1987 and has clearly come a long way in a short time. Essentially, the Online Bible is a software program that allows you to use your computer to study the Bible. Mr. Pierce permits, and even encourages, the Online Bible software and modules to be copied and distributed freely. With the exception of some copyrighted texts, such as the NIV, all Online Bible software and modules are free. You can find the Online Bible software available for download from many Christian BBSs.

Bible translations currently supported by the Online Bible include the 1769 Authorized Version (King James Version), the 1890 Darby Bible, the 1898 Young's Literal Translation, the Revised Standard Version, the New Revised Standard Version, the New International Version, and the 1901 American Standard Version. If those aren't enough, Spanish, French, German, and, of course, Greek and Hebrew versions are also available.

In addition to the many Bible translations, the Online Bible includes Strong's numbers keyed to the Authorized Version, Greek and Hebrew lexicons, Thompson Chain References, *New Topical Textbook, Treasury of Scripture Knowledge, Robertson's Word Pictures of the New Testament, Matthew Henry's Concise Commentary*, Charles Spurgeon's "Morning and Evening" Daily Bible Readings, and numerous other resources. The Online Bible can be run on Macintosh, DOS, Windows, and OS/2 platforms. Currently, new Bible translations or modules are being added at a rate of almost one every other month. A picture of the Online Bible follows on page 81.

Many of the Online Bible modules can be downloaded from local Christian bulletin board systems. Given the large size of the complete package, downloading can take a while. Many Sysops or generous online neighbors may be willing to save you the trouble by copying the software onto floppy disks and mailing it to you. Some Christian BBSs carry the Online Bible discussion group, part of the Christian Distribution Network, which offers technical and general support for the Online Bible. The Online Bible can also be retrieved from the Internet by using FTP (see chapter 11). The PC version is located as **sunsite.unc.edu** in the **/pub/academic/religious_studies/bible** directory, while Mac users can go to **amazon.eng.fau.edu** and look in the **/pub/religion/OLB** directory. Finally, you can order the software on disk or CD-ROM from Online Bible USA at 1-800-243-7124. The CD-ROM complete with the latest versions of all modules and translations currently costs only fifteen dollars. Online

```
Help    Search   Display   Print    Verse List   Notes   Options   Quit
+----------------------------------------------------------------------------+
| Ro 4:7 [Saying], Blessed [are]   | 1 ¶ [There is] therefore now no         |
|   they whose iniquities are      | condemnation to them who are in         |
|   forgiven, and whose sins are   | Christ Jesus, who walk not according    |
|   covered.                       | to the flesh, but according to the      |
| Ro 4:7 'Happy they whose lawless | Spirit.                                 |
|   acts were forgiven, and whose  |   1 ¶ There is, then, now no            |
|   sins were covered;             | condemnation to those in Christ         |
| Ro 4:8 Blessed [is] the man to   | Jesus, who walk not according to the    |
|   whom the Lord will not impute  | flesh, but according to the Spirit;     |
|   sin.                           |   2 For the law of the Spirit of life   |
| Ro 4:8 happy the man to whom the | in Christ Jesus hath made me free       |
|   Lord may not reckon sin.'      | from the law of sin and death.          |
| Ro 5:1 Therefore being justified |   2 for the law of the Spirit of the    |
|   by faith, we have peace with God | life in Christ Jesus did set me free  |
|   through our Lord Jesus Christ: | from the law of the sin and of the      |
| Ro 5:1 Having been declared      | death;                                  |
|   righteous, then, by faith, we  |   3 For what the law could not do, in   |
|   have peace toward God through our | that it was weak through the flesh,  |
|   Lord Jesus Christ,             | God sending his own Son, in the         |
| Ro 7:17 Now then it is no more I | likeness of sinful flesh, and for       |
|   that do it, but sin that dwelleth | sin, condemned sin in the flesh: (for|
+----------------------Ge 1:1 - Re 22:21 AV_YLT/NOTES -   1/27 +=             +
F1 Help          F3 Show Passage F5 Strong's <-> F7 DOS Gateway  F9 Quick Print
F2 Save to List F4 Definition   F6 Version <->  F8 Display Note F10 Cross Refs
```

Bible USA also offers the diskette versions with prices starting at twenty dollars for the basic Authorized Version package. Considering that many commercial packages charge hundreds of dollars for the same functions and resources, the Online Bible is an incredible bargain. If you are looking for Bible software, take advantage of this powerful study tool.

Profile: The On-Line Bible College

The On-Line Bible College (OLBC) is a ministry developed by the Christian International School of Theology (CI). Although CI has been offering undergraduate and graduate programs for over twenty-five years, the OLBC itself is only a few years old. Currently, over eighty classes and twelve different degree programs ranging from a certificate in biblical studies to a doctoral degree in theology are offered. The OLBC is intended to provide a theologically conservative biblical education through distance learning and telecomputing. Rather than compete with regional and denominational seminaries, the OLBC seeks to serve those who might not otherwise be able to receive formal biblical education.

The On-Line Bible College uses the Servant of the Lord Christian BBS in Virginia as its electronic campus. Servant of the Lord is a twenty-four hour, user-friendly BBS that maintains all of the information files about the OLBC. It is also the primary means that students use to communicate with faculty members. While courses taken through the OLBC involve traditional assignment sheets, textbooks, papers, and tests, students complete their assignments on a computer and then upload them to the Servant of the Lord BBS. There they are reviewed and graded by the OLBC instructors. As you might expect, feedback is returned through e-mail.

As the advances in telecommunication technologies are making distance learning more common across the nation, it is encouraging to see Christians capitalizing on the opportunities offered by this new technology. This is not an endorsement of the On-Line Bible College, but a highlight of a far-reaching and potentially invaluable use of online technology for the edification of the church. For further information about the On-Line Bible College, contact the Servant of the Lord BBS at (804) 590-2161 and review or download the OLBC information files. You can also contact the dean, Dr. Charles A. Wootten, by calling Servant of the Lord BBS or through e-mail at the following addresses: `listener1@aol.com`, `76476.1556@compuserve.com`, or `ambx84a@prodigy.com`.

7

Introduction
to the Internet

Considering all of the recent publicity surrounding the Internet, you might be tempted to believe that it is a recent technological advance. Actually, the Internet is over twenty years old and was never intended to be used in the way it is today. This chapter will provide a brief history of the Internet, introduce the different Internet services, and hopefully excite you about the many opportunities available to Internet adventurers.

History of the Internet

In the 1960s the Department of Defense's Advanced Research Projects Agency, known as ARPA, started researching possible ways to interconnect computers located in different geographic areas. This task required developing technologies and standards for both the computers and the communications lines that interconnected them. The Defense Department's primary focus was not efficiency, as you might expect, but tenacity. Since the Cold War was in full swing, there was a genuine concern about how a network would survive if some of its computers were destroyed in an attack. The resulting design was not wholly unlike the postal system.

Essentially, computers take the information to be transmitted over the network, break it into smaller pieces, and place the pieces into a series of electronic envelopes called packets. Each packet contains the address of the sender, the address of the recipient, and other pertinent information. The computer then sends the packets to a neighboring computer that checks the destination address and forwards it on toward the destination. If the computer doesn't know where to send it, or if for some reason the desired phone line or computer is down, the computer directs it along an alternate path. Eventually, the various packets are passed from computer to computer until they reach their destination. At the destination the computer opens the packets, pieces the information back together, and gives it to the user. This whole system, with all of the technical details, became known as the Internet Protocol or IP. An additional protocol was then developed to allow the two end systems to talk to each other and indicate that they either received the data or needed it re-sent. This was called the Transmission Control Protocol or TCP. When coupled together the protocols are referred to as TCP/IP.

The Defense Department's system worked, and the resulting computer network was called the Advanced Research Project Agency Network or ARPAnet. During the 1970s the ARPAnet was used by researchers to exchange information. As time went on, other groups sought to imitate the ARPAnet concept. To assist in this quest, TCP/IP software was combined with UNIX, the major operating system used by corporations and educational institutions at that time. This resulted in the development and proliferation of a variety of smaller TCP/IP networks.

People sought ways of communicating between the various TCP/IP-based networks and computers. They started establishing gateways to enable networks to communicate with one another. This series of interconnected networks became known as the Internet.

Because of the success of such internetworking, the National Science Foundation developed a high-speed backbone network known as the NSFnet during the 1980s. It was designed to facilitate even more usage of the Internet for research purposes. In 1989 the ARPAnet was dismantled, leaving the NSFnet backbone to become the heart of the Internet.

Until the late 1980s and early 1990s, the Internet was used strictly for research and nonprofit purposes. During this time, a TCP/IP network called the Commercial Internet Exchange, or CIX, was developed and integrated into the Internet to allow people to access the Internet for business purposes. Thus, research traffic could flow over the NSFnet backbone while commercial traffic passed through the CIX.

Recently, the National Science Foundation realized that it should no longer be responsible for funding the major Internet backbone (which has expanded well beyond its original purpose of scientific research) and thus phased out the NSFnet. A new architecture has been developed that places a greater emphasis on regional network service providers. Organizations will purchase connections through these regional providers, which will then, in turn, be connected through network access points. These access points will be tied together via a combination of new and existing high-speed backbone links.

With the announcement of the National Information Infrastructure and the development of the information superhighway concept, public use of the Internet has exploded. People who had never heard of the Internet two or three years ago now use it for daily conversations, research, and even business transactions. While estimates of the number of Internet users varies, it is safe to say that at least 35 million people access the Internet in one form or another.

How Do I Subscribe to the Internet?

In short, you don't. The Internet is not a closed system like Prodigy or CompuServe. Actually, you could loosely define the Internet as the worldwide sum total of all computers and networks that are interconnected to one another using the TCP/IP protocol. Defining the Internet is as difficult as defining the boundaries of the nationwide road system. That system is the sum total of all of the highways, freeways, beltways, and other roads which are interconnected. You don't join the highway system; you just drive on it. In the same way, you don't subscribe to the Internet; you just connect to it. That's why this book introduced you to commercial online services and UNIX accounts before explaining the details of the Internet.

What Can I Do on the Internet?

Because of the size of the Internet, and because it has a long information-sharing history, the vast multitude of resources it contains is simply astounding. Just imagine being able to send prayer requests to friends in Hungary, Hawaii, and Houston and get responses back the same day. How about getting a free copy of Polycarp's letter to the Philippians and then discussing it with experts on the early church fathers? Perhaps you want to search the Library of Congress card catalog while sitting in your pajamas. Would you like to look at photographs of the Dead Sea Scrolls or read the catalog of a local seminary or Bible college? Maybe you would like a free subscription to an electronic magazine about contemporary Christian music. Whatever your interests are, you will probably find something about them on the Internet. Once you become familiar with the Internet, you will have a difficult time imagining life without it.

Internet Services

Contrary to popular opinion, you don't just connect to the Internet and access information the same way that you would on a commercial online service. There is no Internet Main Menu or opening screen. Navigating the Internet actually means using a variety of Internet services such as e-mail and Gopher. Let's briefly summarize these Internet services, which will be examined in greater detail in the forthcoming chapters.

The most common use of the Internet is electronic mail. You have the ability to send e-mail to Internet users all over the globe. Soon you will be teaching your children their Internet address in addition to their street address. Typical Internet addresses look like this: `julianne@trowe.com`, `laurab@watson.ibm.com`, or `bakerbooks@aol.com`.

The next most popular Internet service is probably USENET. USENET is a gigantic, worldwide collection of discussion groups much like the topical discussion groups, or forums, found on commercial online services and Christian bulletin board systems. The difference is one of magnitude. While commercial services and BBSs may have tens or hundreds of discussion groups, USENET has thousands of groups, and new ones are created daily.

Some Internet tools actually allow you to directly access other computers on the Internet. One of these is Telnet. Telnet is useful if you have more than one account that you need to log in to or if you want to find information running on a publicly accessible computer system. FTP is another tool that accesses other computers. Rather than logging on as a user, FTP allows you to connect to a computer for the purpose of transferring files. FTP can be a real treat as you seek to expand your own personal library of computer and other resources.

Gopher is a more recent service that provides a menu or tree structure by which you can browse various computers for particular resources. One of the things that makes Gopher popular is that you don't need to know specific Internet addresses and technical jargon, so you can just focus on research. Gopher is one of the services making the Internet more accessible to those who do not like traditional UNIX commands.

One of the newest Internet services is called the World Wide Web. WWW is a service that allows you to set up hypertext links between different information pages throughout the Internet. Hypertext is a means of linking various topics together based on common key words. The Web is like Gopher in that you don't have to know where everything is located, but rather than using a hierarchical menu structure, navigation in the WWW can follow a multitude of paths.

Since the Internet is a dynamic entity, other tools have already come and gone, and more can be expected to come in the future. The tools mentioned above are the most widely used Internet services and the ones that you should know in order to maximize your Internet experience.

Unfortunately not every Internet provider offers every Internet service. Remember the overview table in chapter 4? Different commercial on-line services include various levels of Internet support. Furthermore, even if you get a UNIX shell account there is no guarantee that your provider will support all of the above-mentioned services. Be sure to ask what services are available before you sign up with an online provider.

8

Electronic Mail

In the 1800s the Pony Express made headlines by delivering mail from Missouri to California in ten days. During the 1980s, Federal Express became a corporate success delivering packages anywhere in the world overnight. Electronic mail, however, can traverse thousands of miles in a matter of seconds—one of the primary reasons that it has become so popular. You can literally sit in a kitchen in Baltimore and send a message to your grandparents in Berlin. Best of all, Grandma can read the letter minutes after it's sent. It's no wonder that e-mail has become the preferred method of communication for millions of Internet users.

Internet Addresses

Address Format

Much like the postal system, everyone on the Internet has a unique mailing address. Both types of addresses consist of a person's name followed by some information which identifies where that particular person is located. Before examining an electronic mailing address, let's review a normal post office address. A postal address has the following form:

Name
Street Address
City, State Zip

So a typical address would look like:

Dave Smith
555 Oak Lane
Meadowville, PA 20871

This tells the post office that they are to send the letter to Mr. Dave Smith who lives at 555 Oak Lane in the city of Meadowville, in the state of Pennsylvania, in the area assigned with the zip code 20871. So even though there might be five thousand Dave Smiths in the world, the post office will only deliver the letter to the Dave Smith living on Oak Lane in Meadowville, Pennsylvania.

An Internet mailing address serves the same function. Internet addresses are typically of the following form:

`username@network.organization.type`

Note that the address fits on a single line, does not contain spaces, and uses periods to separate different sections of information. The username, which can be a variation of a person's given name or initials, is the name of the recipient's computer account. The @ or *at* sign simply separates the user's name from his or her address, much like starting a new line for someone's street address. The network name, if present, identifies a specific computer network at a particular organization. While not all addresses have this network portion, it helps to pinpoint the recipient. Finally, like the zip code, the type extension identifies the kind of location to which you are writing. For the sake of brevity the `network.organization.type` sequence is often known as the domain name. Thus an Internet address could be restated as:

`username@domainname`

Although e-mail addresses may at first appear cryptic, it won't take long for you to be as familiar with your electronic address as you are with your street address. Let's examine a few examples:

`dsmith@saturn.eastern.edu`
`xrwy93a@prodigy.com`
`vice-president@whitehouse.gov`

Using the first example, the address `dsmith@saturn.eastern.edu` tells the mailing system to send the message to a user named `dsmith` who is located on the **saturn** network at Eastern College. While there might be five hundred **dsmith** accounts on the Internet, only one is located at **saturn.eastern.edu**. The second address is an example of a **.com** extension, which usually denotes a company, in this case Prodigy. The final example, the only real Internet address listed, is actually the Internet e-mail address for the vice president of the United States.

It's important to realize that you need someone's complete address for electronic mail to get through. You cannot send e-mail to **tbecker** and assume that the Internet will figure out that you are referring to Tina Becker at Bethany Christian Services and not Tom Becker at Apple Computer. If you type in an erroneous destination address, your mail will "bounce back" to you with a message indicating that no such user exists. Essentially, it is an electronic version of the "return to sender, address unknown" stamp placed on incorrectly addressed envelopes. Unlike the postal system, your mail will not get forwarded to you if you change your Internet address.

Have you noticed that all of the addresses have been written in lowercase type? Although most systems don't care whether you send mail to **bmullikin@wheaton.edu** or **BMULLIKIN@WHEATON.EDU**, lowercase is the standard.

Address Types

In the previous set of examples you saw e-mail addresses with type extensions of **edu**, **com**, and **gov**. Most addresses within the United States use one of the following location types:

Type	Meaning	Type	Meaning
.com	Companies or businesses	.mil	Military
.edu	Educational institutions	.net	Network providers
.gov	Government	.org	Nonprofit organizations

Often, a country code is appended to an address which originates outside of the United States. Common country codes include the following:

Code	Country	Code	Country
.au	Australia	.fr	France
.ca	Canada	.mx	Mexico
.de	Germany	.se	Sweden
.fi	Finland	.uk	United Kingdom

For example, Ms. Alice Wysong, working for Christian Computer Corporation's Paris, France, office, might have an e-mail address that looks like this: `awysong@cccorp.com.fr`.

Finding Other People

It is estimated that over 35 million people are connected to the Internet. Major corporations, small companies, universities, churches, executives, farmers, pastors, housewives, and missionaries all converse through e-mail. Unfortunately, there is not a master phone book listing the names of all 35 million people and where to contact them. (Perhaps one may be developed, but it isn't here yet.) Therefore, figuring out the address of a person that you want to write to is often your biggest challenge.

If a person with whom you would like to communicate is on the same commercial service or Internet provider as you, then you may be able to search a master address list containing all current subscribers. If, however, you want to communicate with someone on a different service, then you must find other means to locate their address.

The most effective way to find out someone's Internet address is to ask for it. While it may seem strange to make a phone call to find out where to send an electronic letter, it is often the simplest way. If someone sends you a letter via the Internet, you can also discover their address by examining the From: line in the header of the message. By the way, if you don't know your own Internet address, just ask the system administrator or support person for your computer service.

Finger

Another way of locating someone is by using a command called Finger. Finger allows you to query another computer system for information about a particular user. A generic Finger command could be described as follows:

```
finger user@network.organization.type or
finger user@organization.type
```

The catch, of course, is that you first need to know the user's domain name. For instance, suppose you wanted to find the Internet address of Steve Kelly at Messiah College, and you knew that Messiah's Internet domain name was **@messiah.edu**. You could enter:

```
finger steve@messiah.edu or
finger kelly@messiah.edu
```

If Messiah College set up their system with a phone book feature that permits such requests, it might respond to **finger kelly@messiah.edu** with a message such as:

```
Kelly Baliko      kbaliko@love.messiah.edu
Steve Kelly       skelly@peace.messiah.edu
Kelly Zeiler      kzeiler@love.messiah.edu
```

You would then know that Steve's Internet address was **skelly@peace.messiah.edu**. Notice that it listed all of the users on the **@messiah.edu** domain who had the name Kelly.

Let's look at a successful Finger sequence performed on a typical UNIX shell account. For this example, we are looking for Elsie Crane at the fictional Christian Theological Seminary. We already know that CTS's domain name is **cts.edu**.

```
explorer:[/opt2/usr/rsteel] finger crane@cts.edu
[cts.edu]
Searching phonebook from tulip.cts.edu for "crane" ...

MailName            Name and Department/Class Year
----------------------------------------------------------------
crane@cts.edu       Crane Curtis C              Class of '93
ecrane@cts.edu      Crane Elsie Dennis          Class of '96
gcrane@cts.edu      Crane George William        Class of '95
tcrane@cts.edu      Crane Thomas Kennedy        Class of '98

explorer:[/opt2/usr/rsteel]
```

Since many organizations don't operate a phone book system, your Finger request might fail. A failure might look like this:

```
explorer:[/opt2/usr/rsteel] finger crane@cts.edu
[cts.edu]
?Sorry, could not find "CRANE"

explorer:[/opt2/usr/rsteel]
```

If you Finger the exact Internet address of someone (such as **ecrane@cts.edu**), you might also discover when they last logged on, if they have any unread mail, and even a message known as a plan. A plan is simply a greeting message included by some users. Take note of the various information provided to the seeker:

```
explorer:[/opt2/usr/rsteel] finger ecrane@cts.edu
[cts.edu]
ECRANE       Elsie D. Crane       ECRANE not logged in
Last login Tue 31-Jan-95 8:47PM-EDT

Plan:

To do justly
To love mercy
And to walk humbly with my God

explorer:[/opt2/usr/rsteel]
```

Remember, not all computer systems have the Finger capability; thus, you will not always receive a response to a Finger inquiry.

Whois

Another search method is the Whois command. You use Whois when you don't know someone's username or domain name. Whois searches a large list of Internet addresses and attempts to match your request. The generic form of the command looks like this:

whois user *or*
whois organization

Although the vast majority of users are not listed in the Whois database, most organizations are. So let's say that you wanted to find Jimmie McKee at Calvin College. If you attempted:

whois mckee

you probably wouldn't find his address. However you could type:

whois calvin college

and learn that Calvin College has an Internet domain name of calvin.edu. With that information you could then use the Finger command by typing:

```
finger mckee@calvin.edu
```

Thus, by combining the Whois and Finger commands, you can make significant headway into finding someone's Internet address.

Some Internet providers may not have the Whois software running on their system. If you don't get a suitable response when attempting the Whois command, you can also access the Internet's NIC by using Telnet. From a UNIX shell account you would issue the following command:

```
telnet rs.internic.net
```

Telnet is a way of connecting to another Internet computer and will be explained further in chapter 10. Essentially, if you Telnet to **rs.internic.net** you will be able to use the Whois command.

Gopher and World Wide Web

Many colleges and universities connected to the Internet have placed searchable e-mail directories of their students and faculty on their Gopher and World Wide Web servers. Once you find such a directory you can typically search the whole school by name or display addresses of those in a particular department.

If you are using Gopher, look through the geographic hierarchy until you locate the desired school. Once there, simply examine the menu and see if they offer a searchable directory. If you have access to the Web, using either a graphical browser like Netscape or a text browser such a Lynx, you stand an even greater chance of finding someone. Point your browser to the school's Web page, usually at **http://www.organization.type**, and look for an e-mail directory. An alphabetical list of colleges and universities on the Web can be found at **http://www.mit.edu:8001/people/ cdemello/univ.html**. Additional information about Gopher and the World Wide Web is found in chapters 12 and 13 respectively.

Postmasters

Yet another way of locating someone is by sending a note to a user named postmaster. Typically every site on the Internet has at least one person assigned as the postmaster to handle various mailing issues. To keep things simple, their username is **postmaster**, and their address would look like this:

postmaster@network.organization.type *or*
postmaster@organization.type

For example, the postmaster for George Fox College would be:

postmaster@foxmail.gfc.edu

Postmasters are typically *very* busy people who don't have the time to hunt for e-mail addresses. Therefore, use the postmaster only as a last resort. If you do send a note to the postmaster asking about someone's address, he or she will probably respond to your request or forward it to the person about whom you have asked. The latter method is done to protect the privacy of the users.

Sending Mail to Different Online Services

Often you may want to send electronic mail to someone who uses America Online, Delphi, or some other online service. The following list contains a number of major online services and the domain name associated with each. Before you can send mail to someone on one of these online services, you will need to know the person's username on that system. Note that some services use actual names for usernames while others use numbers. To send Internet mail simply substitute the recipient's username in place of the word **username**:

Service	*Address*
America Online	**username@aol.com**
ATT Mail	**username@attmail.com**
Bitnet[1]	**username@useraddress.bitnet**
Bix	**username@bix.com**
CompuServe[2]	**username@compuserve.com**
Delphi	**username@delphi.com**
Fidonet[3]	**user.name@pd.fc.nb.za.fidonet.org**
GEnie	**username@genie.geis.com**
MCI Mail	**username@mcimail.com**
Netcom	**username@netcom.com**
Portal	**username@cup.portal.com**
Prodigy	**username@prodigy.com**

1. Bitnet addresses typically look like **username@useraddress**. Therefore just add **.bitnet** to the end. So **rshearer@buvax** would be **rshearer@buvax.bitnet**

2. Note that in the CompuServe username, the comma is changed to a period when sending Internet mail. Thus user **12345,678** becomes **12345.678@compuserve.com**

3. A Fidonet username includes the person's first and last name and a numerical Fidonet address in the form **a:b/c.d**. Hence when you send mail from the Internet you put a period between the person's first and last name and substitute the appropriate numbers for **a**, **b**, **c**, and **d**. For example, **Sandy Rowe** at **4:2/9.1** would be **sandy.rowe@p1.f9.n2.z4.fidonet.org**

Mailing Systems

Each online provider has its own particular interface for sending mail. Such interfaces are known as mailing systems or mailers, and they come in a variety of styles. Some have graphical icons where you click on a mailbox to send a note, while others are text-based and require you to type the **mail** or **send** command. Because each system is different, it is difficult to document a one-size-fits-all approach to e-mail. However, all mailers allow you to read e-mail messages, send messages, and store messages for later viewing.

Graphical Mailers

Figure 12 shows a picture of the AOL graphical mailer. Notice the friendly icons that accompany the letter's different parts. In order to send mail, simply fill in the destination and subject fields, write the actual message, and click on the Send Now icon to mail the note.

Other graphical mailers, such as the ones found on Prodigy and CompuServe WinCIM, are similar. There really aren't any commands to memorize; just fill in the blanks and click the appropriate icons.

Text-Based Mailers

UNIX mailers are a bit different because they are text-based. The basic UNIX mailer is actually called Mail. Unfortunately, the Mail package is not very friendly. Two of the more common UNIX mailers are Elm and Pine. You can run these mailing systems by typing **elm** or **pine**, respectively, at the UNIX system prompt. Since Pine is based on Elm, the two systems are quite similar. We will look at Pine as it is easier for a beginner to use.

When you first run Pine you are presented with a number of options including Compose a Message, Folder List, and Folder Index. Compose a Message allows you to write and send e-mail, Folder List prompts you to

Figure 12

America
Online
Mailer

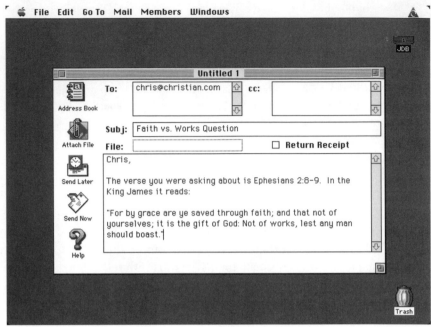

select a specific mail folder (such as inbox or sent-mail), and Folder Index lists the contents of a previously selected folder. You can choose one of these options by typing the appropriate letter highlighted in the menu or by using the up and down arrow keys to move the cursor to your choice and hitting Return.

If you would like to read mail with Pine, choose the Folder Index option, by pressing **I**, from the main menu. Inbox, the default folder, is where e-mail is stored until you delete or move selected messages. The following picture shows a typical folder index:

```
   PINE 3.91 FOLDER INDEX                Folder: INBOX Message 1 of 12
-----------------------------------------------------------------------------

+   1   Aug 27 C.J. Colaianni      (2,048) CD-ROM Access / Linux CD
+ A 2   Aug 28 Delphi Internet Se  (1,630) Re: Re-Subscribing to Delphi
+   3   Aug 28 Delphi Internet Se (11,557) Re: Re-Subscribing to Delphi
+ A 4   Aug 31 The Whooping Crane  (2,630) Re: Hey Cranium
+ A 5   Aug 31 The Whooping Crane  (1,272) Re: Hey Cranium
+ A 6   Sep  1 BakerBooks@aol.com    (761) Re: Welcome!
+ A 7   Sep  2 teggleston@bell.com (1,673) The New Season
        8   Sep  3 archive-server@jus (10,635) Slackpro information
```

```
+ A 9    Sep  6 todd@dworshak.com    (1,809) RE: New Job
+ A 10   Sep  6 BakerBooks@aol.com   (2,120) Re: Welcome!
     11  Sep  6 mrose@harding.edu    (1,771) New School Year
+ A 12   Sep  7 BakerBooks@aol.com   (1,553) Re: Welcome!


                     [Last Index page]
--------------------------------------------------------------
? Help          M Main Menu  P PrevMsg—PrevPage      D Delete    R Reply
O OTHER CMDS    V [ViewMsg]  N NextMsg  Spc NextPage  U Undelete  F Forward
```

Pine is created, trademarked, and copyrighted by the University of Washington.

As you can see, the index presents a list of messages in the order that they were received. Information about who sent the message, when it was sent, and the subject are also shown. You then have a number of options including viewing, deleting, or responding to particular messages. Notice that the various options are listed at the bottom of the screen. Take note of the ? choice which can be selected to display Pine's excellent online help feature.

In order to send a message, you first choose Compose Mail from the main menu. After filling in the To and Subject fields, you can then write your message. Pine uses a full-screen editor, which means that you can make corrections to your message anywhere by using the arrow keys to move around and then adding or deleting information. The following shows an e-mail message composed with the Pine mailer:

```
  PINE 3.91   COMPOSE MESSAGE              Folder: INBOX 12 Messages
--------------------------------------------------------------------------

To      : bakerbooks@aol.com
Cc      :
Attchmnt:
Subject : New Catalog
----- Message Text -----

Would you please send me the new catalog listing the latest releases
from Baker Book House? I heard that you now have the list online.
Please send it to ericm@cts.edu. Thank you.

Eric Molicki
ericm@cts.org


--------------------------------------------------------------------------
^G Get Help ^X Send    ^R Read File ^Y Prev Pg ^K Cut Text   ^O Postpone
^C Cancel   ^J Justify ^W Where is  ^V Next Pg ^U UnCut Text ^T To Spell
```

The ^ symbol is shorthand for the Control key, so ^X actually means to press the Control and **X** keys at the same time. As you can see from the menu, Control-**X** will send your message.

To learn more about the particular mailer available from your online computer service, read the online help or ask the system operator, postmaster, or another user. Once you get into your mailer, practice by sending yourself a few messages. This will help you become familiar with the e-mail process and perhaps save you some headaches.

Anatomy of an E-Mail Message

When you receive an e-mail message you will notice its two main components: a header followed by the message text or body. An example of an Internet e-mail message is shown below:

Header

```
From chris@mason.edu Jul 29, 95 06:32:48 pm est
Date: Sat, 29 Jul 95 18:32:48 EST
To: colin@mason.edu
Subject: Dinner Request
```

Body

```
Can you come over for dinner tomorrow night? Let me know.
Thanks.

Chris
chris@mason.edu
```

In this example, the first four lines constitute the header of the message. An e-mail header, similar to a memo header, traditionally consists of the author's address, the recipient's address, the subject, and the date and time received. Some mailing systems will also add to the header information about the path that the message took from the sender to the receiver. Others will strip away the header entirely. The actual e-mail message then follows the header. At the bottom of the note is a signature block, which in this example consists of the author's name and Internet e-mail address.

Pine, like most mail readers, allows you to reply to a message with a single command. When you type **R** from the Folder Index, the mailer will automatically address your e-mail reply to the sender of the original note.

Expressing Yourself in E-Mail

E-Mail Etiquette

E-mail is a great form of communication, but you need to be careful when using it. Be aware that some online services require you to sign an agreement that basically gives a system operator the right to read any e-mail messages that you send or receive. A few even edit notes to remove offensive language. Therefore, do not put anything in an e-mail message that you wouldn't want others to see. Always consider the consequences if someone other than the addressee reads the note.

Remember, also, that both upper- and lowercase letters should be used in your note. Some new users write messages in all uppercase, AND IT GETS VERY DIFFICULT TO READ LETTERS WRITTEN LIKE THIS. Besides being difficult to read, all capitals makes it appear that you are SHOUTING! Also, remember that people cannot read body language in your messages, so be careful to say precisely what you mean.

When writing an e-mail message, it is considered polite to include a signature at the bottom of the message. Since Internet addresses can often be buried in a long header, adding your signature to the message makes it easier for the reader to identify you. A good signature is no more than four lines long and includes your name, Internet address, and any other relevant (or witty) information that you choose to include. If you have a UNIX shell account, you can automate your signature program by editing a file called .signature (yes, with the period). Once updated, the contents of the .signature file will automatically be appended to any message that you send.

Many mailers allow you to reply to a message while including the original message in the letter. Notice:

```
From colin@mason.edu  Jul 29, 95 9:22:42 pm est
Date: Sat, 29 Jul 95 21:22:42 EST
To: chris@mason.edu
Subject: Re: Dinner Request

>Can you come over for dinner tomorrow night? Let me know.

Sorry, but I'm booked all day tomorrow. I'm free on Tuesday night, could we
reschedule?

>Chris

Colin
colin@mason.edu
```

Note how part of the old letter is set off with > symbols? This is considered acceptable as long as you don't include too much of the old message. The best policy is to include only as much of the old letter as you need to make your point.

Conveying Emotions

One of the challenges of online communication is trying to convey emotions in messages that have neither pictures nor sound. To complicate matters, most mail systems do not enable you to use bold, italics, or underline. Fortunately, there are a few standard conventions that allow you to rise above these restrictions.

Asterisks are frequently used in place of bold or italic type to emphasize a point. If you wrote a note saying "I *really* want you to call me tonight," you are emphasizing the word *really* much like you would punctuate that word in a spoken request. Pointed brackets are often used to describe body language. For instance, if you wrote a message saying "It's okay that you can't make the party <sigh>," then you are showing your regret at the negative reply. For happy occasions, <g> or <grin> and <bg> mean grin and big grin, respectively. In order to signify an underline, it is common to place lines at the beginning and end of a word or phrase. Thus, a book title might be written _Moby Dick_ to signify that it should be underlined.

Characters can also be arranged to symbolize an emotional feeling. These arrangements are known as *emoticons*—a word created by combining *emotion* with *icons*. Sometimes they express true feelings, while other times they are used sarcastically. A few common emoticons are shown below. (Tilt your head 90 degrees to the left to recognize them.)

Emoticon	Meaning
:-)	Happy
8-)	Happy
;-)	Winking
:(	Sad
:-(	Sad
:-0	Surprised

Keep an eye out; people come up with some pretty creative symbols. Would you believe that =|:-) is a man wearing a top hat, 0:-) is an angel, and 8(:-) is a woman wearing Mickey Mouse ears? Maybe you can design a unique one for your signature line. See if you can figure out the meaning of this one: ><

Mailing Lists

There are literally hundreds of Internet mailing lists that you can join. These range from active discussions to informational notes sent to you on a regular basis. While the topics range from football teams to theater, there are a number of mailing lists that are particularly relevant to Christians. Joining a mailing list is easy; simply send an e-mail message to the specified address and request that your name be added to the list. You may cancel at any time by sending a cancel request.

Some mailing lists are processed automatically. Rather than having a person sort through all of the requests, a computer program reads the requests and automatically adds each sender to the desired mailing list. Common automated mailing list systems include Listserv, Mailserv, Listproc, and Majordomo. If you are told to subscribe to a mailing list by sending a note to an account called **listserv**, such as **listserv@christian.com**, then you know that you are working with an automated system.

Let's look at an example. Suppose our friend Chris Christian wanted to join the Christian Literature list. Chris knew from appendix C that the list was called **christlit** and the request address was **listserv@bethel.edu**. The request message would resemble:

```
To : listserv@bethel.edu
Cc :
Attchmnt:
Subject :
----- Message Text -----

subscribe christlit Chris Christian
```

Notice that the message body consists of the **subscribe** command, the name of the mailing list, and Chris's name. The following chart lists common Listserv commands:

Command	Purpose
subscribe *listname yourname*	Subscribe yourself to the list called *listname*
unsubscribe *listname yourname*	Cancel subscription to *listname*
info *listname*	Request the introductory information for *listname*
help	Request Listserv command assistance

Thus, using Listserv, Chris can quit the list by substituting the command **unsubscribe** in the same message. As you can see, Listservs are not very complicated. Other automated systems may have slightly different commands, but the basic procedure remains the same.

Where to Begin

One particularly interesting resource available through e-mail is an electronic edition of a magazine called *The Lighthouse*. The Lighthouse Electronic Magazine (TLeM) is all about contemporary Christian music and includes reviews, interviews, and news from the CCM industry. The magazine is quite professional. If you are interested in CCM, you can get an electronic subscription to TLeM by sending a note to:

`listserv@netcentral.net`

with a one-line message that says:

`subscribe lighthouse-list Chris Christian`

Substitute your name in place of Chris Christian's.

For those of a more scholarly inclination, the Apologetics mailing list might be of interest. It views the Bible as the authoritative Word of God, and those who participate in discussions abide by that premise. You can subscribe to the Apologetics list by sending a one-line message to

`majordomo@netcom.com`

that reads:

`subscribe apologia-l`

Additional Christian mailing lists, along with details about how to subscribe, are included in the Christian Internet Directory (appendix C).

9

USENET
Newsgroups

In today's individualistic and isolated culture, people have often lamented the demise of old town squares and local pubs, stating, "If only there was a place that folks could gather and just talk about what's on their minds . . ." Well, if you are willing to venture into the world of cyberspace, you will find a modern equivalent known as USENET. Imagine the opportunity to participate in over ten thousand different discussion groups with millions of people around the world. If the idea intrigues you, then you will enjoy USENET.

What Is USENET?

USENET is a collection of thousands of discussion groups that are distributed among computers on the Internet. These groups allow participation in numerous international discussions on a wide variety of topics. Many users prefer USENET groups to mailing lists. This is because you can personally select messages that are of interest; therefore, you don't have to worry about your mailbox overflowing with notes.

Some people mistakenly think that USENET is the Internet. It is not; USENET is merely one type of information that is distributed over the Internet. Be aware that there is no central USENET computer. Multiple systems, networked together, propagate new information as it is received. Eventually, the information fans out to all of the computers that subscribe to USENET groups. The process is not unlike the way that computer bulletin board systems exchange forum information. While BBSs often do their information exchanges at 2:00 A.M., Internet computers are constantly comparing their USENET messages and copying them as needed.

Although USENET is sometimes called Network News, Internet Newsgroups, or Net News, its discussion groups are not limited to news-type items. There are USENET discussion groups for virtually every conceivable topic. You name it, you can find it—baseball, poetry, heavy metal music, Republicans, food, chemistry, job openings, computers for sale. Some USENET groups are moderated, while others, including virtually all of the "alternative" groups, are unmoderated. A moderator, or referee, so to speak, screens all of the posts made to a newsgroup to ensure that they remain on topic and are not improper. When you send a message to a moderated group, the message must be approved by the moderator before it gets displayed for the general public. Sometimes this approval process will take a few hours or even a few days, so be patient! Unmoderated groups lack such a referee, so posts appear much quicker. The problem with unmoderated groups is that they often wander off track, sometimes becoming downright chaotic. Whether a group is moderated or not, remember to be courteous and respectful. More about USENET etiquette will be discussed in a later section.

Identifying USENET Groups

In order to make USENET more manageable, its groups are arranged in a hierarchical fashion. The following diagram depicts such an arrangement:

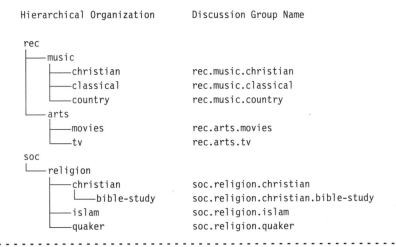

```
Hierarchical Organization          Discussion Group Name

rec
 ├──music
 │    ├──christian               rec.music.christian
 │    ├──classical               rec.music.classical
 │    └──country                 rec.music.country
 └──arts
      ├──movies                  rec.arts.movies
      └──tv                      rec.arts.tv
soc
 └──religion
      ├──christian               soc.religion.christian
      │    └──bible-study        soc.religion.christian.bible-study
      ├──islam                   soc.religion.islam
      └──quaker                  soc.religion.quaker
```

A discussion group's name is determined by its location on the hierarchical tree. For example, `rec.music.christian` is part of the `rec` hierarchy. **Rec** is a category that denotes recreational activities. It is followed by the first major subgroup, **music**, and then by the extension **christian**, indicating a specific group dealing with Christian music. Subscribing would further reveal that `rec.music.christian` is a group primarily dedicated to discussing contemporary Christian music and performers. Other groups within the `rec.music` hierarchy are `rec.music.classical`, `rec.music.country`, and `rec.music.reggae`. As with other UNIX commands, the newsgroups all use lowercase letters.

Most newsgroups can be traced back to one of several root levels, called parent categories. Keeping in mind that not every computer system carries every newsgroup or even every category, here are the primary parent groups with some words of explanation.

Group	Description of Hierarchy
alt	Alternative newsgroups (Be aware that many are adult-oriented and of questionable taste)
comp	Computer-related subjects
misc	Miscellaneous groups that don't fit in the other categories
news	News and discussions about USENET
rec	Recreational activities
sci	Groups about science and research
soc	Discussions about social issues
talk	Discussions and debates about politics and other controversial topics

Be aware that numerous other parent groups do exist. Many focus on geographical locations or special topics. A few of these are listed as examples.

Group	Description of Hierarchy
bionet	Biology-oriented groups
biz	Business-oriented groups
chile	Chile newsgroups
dc	Washington D.C. area groups
eunet	EuNet European groups
k12	Education groups dealing with grades K–12
nc	Groups targeting North Carolina
utexas	University of Texas groups

Newsreaders

By now you are probably starting to realize that every Internet service has a unique interface used to access it. (Actually, the graphical interface Mosaic can act as a front-end for all of the major Internet services. It will be further profiled in chapter 13.) To access USENET you'll need a newsreader.

Commercial Online Services

Commercial online services that carry USENET groups have their own USENET newsreaders. Typically, they allow you to subscribe to newsgroups in three ways. One method is to choose successive hierarchical levels until you find the group that you want. This is a good way to become familiar with the various groups and their locations. Another option is to search for a group based on a particular key word. For instance, a search for the key word *Christian* might reveal:

```
rec.music.christian
soc.religion.christian
soc.religion.christian.bible-study
soc.religion.christian.youth-work
misc.education.home-school.christian
```

Figure 13

CompuServe
CIM
USENET
Newsreader

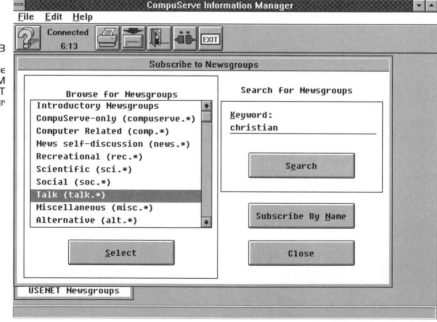

The third way to view a newsgroup is to request it specifically. Of course, this requires that you know the precise name of the newsgroup that you want. A picture of the CompuServe Information Manager's USENET newsreader is shown in figure 13. Notice how you can browse through the hierarchy or search for a newsgroup based on a keyword.

UNIX

If you access the Internet with a UNIX shell, a number of newsreaders, including Nn, Rn, Tin, Trn, and Strn, are available. For beginners, Tin, with its user-friendly menus, good explanations, and online help, is probably the best choice. As with other UNIX programs, Tin can be run simply by typing tin at the command line. Tin will list all of the newsgroups that you subscribe to along with brief descriptions of each, as shown below:

```
          Group Selection (168.143.0.2 33)                h=help

1         news.announce.newusers           Explanatory postings
2     60  misc.forsale                     Short forsale postings
3    156  misc.writing                     Discussion of writing
4      8  misc.education.home-school.christian  Christian home-schooling
5     15  news.answers                     Periodic USENET info posts
6     50  rec.music.christian              Christian music
7     51  rec.arts.disney                  Discussion of Disney
8      4  misc.education                   Discussion of education
9      2  alt.education.home-school.christian  Christian home-schoolers
10     2  comp.os.ms-windows.announce      Windows Announcements
11   144  soc.religion.christian           Christianity
12    89  soc.religion.christian.bible-study  Examining the Holy Bible
13       christnet.christianlife           Applied Christianity
14    17  soc.religion.christian.youth-work  Christians working w/youth
15    85  alt.messianic                    Messianic traditions
16    19  alt.music.amy-grant              Discussion about Amy Grant

   <n>=set current to n, TAB=next unread, /=search pattern, c)atchup,
 g)oto, j=line down, k=line up, h)elp, m)ove, q)uit, r=toggle all/unread,
   s)ubscribe, S)ub pattern, u)nsubscribe, U)nsub pattern, y)ank in/out
```

In the second column from the left, you can see the number of messages in each group that haven't been read yet. Notice also that there is a command menu at the bottom, along with an option to read the online help information. Once you feel comfortable navigating through USENET, you may want to try Trn or Strn, as they are more powerful (but also more cryptic).

You may be wondering about subscribing to USENET groups. Since there are thousands of groups available, reading all of them would be unwieldy. Most newsreaders allow you to choose the groups that interest you and ignore the countless messages that you don't care to read. Be aware, however, that a few newsreaders subscribe you to everything by default. If this is the case then you will have to unsubscribe to the ones that you don't want. Fortunately, most readers allow you to unsubscribe to everything with one command or menu option and then go back and add the groups of your choice.

If you use Tin, complete the following sequence the *first* time Tin is run to ensure that you don't get irrevocably subscribed to all USENET groups:

-Type `tin news.announce.newusers`

(Tin will run with only the `news.announce.newusers` group selected.)

- Type `s`

(You are now subscribed to this group.)

- Type `q`

(Quits Tin.)

Whenever you run Tin, subsequent to the above procedure, simply type `tin` and press Return. The following commands will be of assistance as you subscribe to additional newsgroups:

Command	Purpose
y	Toggles a listing of all USENET groups. Press y to "yank in" the listing when you want to subscribe to new groups. Once you have completed your subscription list, press **y** to "yank out," or remove, the unsubscribed groups
/	Search for groups by keyword
g	Go to a specific group by name
s	Subscribe to a selected group
u	Unsubscribe to a selected group

Reading Messages

Once you have subscribed to your USENET groups, you will be informed of the number of messages that you haven't read in each group. To begin reading, simply select a group. You will then be presented with a list of the subject headings for each unread message. The following picture shows such a selection using Tin. Notice that some message topics, called threads, have multiple postings (as seen by the second number from the left):

```
        soc.religion.christian (87T 144A OK OH R)   h=help

33  + 2   On what happened to the Dinosaurs        petewest@aol.com
34  +     The Bible and Evangelism                  Tom Wimsatt
35  + 2   Jews and Christians                       Joe Rudden
36  +     Keeping the Sabbath                       Dick Wiedenheft
37  +     Jehovah's Witnesses & Christ's Divinity   Tracy Smith
38  +     Sonship Question                          Julianne Baker
39  +     Revival in China                          Mike Curtis
40  +     Parenting and the Bible                   Scott Radcliffe
41  +     Natural Law                               laurab@vnova.edu
42  + 2   What about Hebrews 6?                     cyn808@udel.edu
43  +     Sermon by Martin Luther                   dad@aol.com
44  +     Ecology and Genesis                       Jennifer Pearson
45  + 2   Worship and the Bible                     RON GAVLIN
46  + 3   Question: Predestination vs. Free Will    David Vosseller
47  + 5   What Adam and Eve do before the fall?     Lynn Firestine
48  +     Origins of Praise Music?                  James Lowe - jlowe

<n>=set current to n, TAB=next unread, /=search pattern, ^K)ill/select,
a)uthor search, c)atchup, j=line down, k=line up, K=mark read, l)ist thread,
|=pipe, m)ail, o=print, q)uit, r=toggle all/unread, s)ave, t)ag, w=post
```

Finally, select the particular message(s) that you want to view, and read away! A typical newsgroup posting is shown below:

```
Article 20753 of soc.religion.christian:
From: jcb@chapelgate.org (Julianne Baker)
Newsgroups: soc.religion.christian
Subject: Sonship Question
Followup-To: soc.religion.christian
Date: Mon Feb 6 16:37:14 EDT 1995
Organization: Chapelgate Church
Lines: 7
Distribution: world

Does anyone have any information about the Sonship material from World Harvest
Mission? My church is going to have a Sonship conference next month and I
wanted to learn more about it. Thanks for your assistance.

Julianne
jcb@chapelgate.org
```

As you can see, a newsgroup posting bears a striking resemblance to an e-mail message. Essentially, it's an e-mail message that can be viewed by millions of people. There is a header containing information such as the address of the poster, the newsgroup that the message has been posted in, and the subject of the posting.

After reading a message you will have a number of options including posting a response to the message, going on to the next message, searching for messages by a keyword, or catching up on any unread messages. The catch-up feature is particularly useful. Let's say that there are fifty new messages since you last read a group. After reading the five or six that interest you, you can "catch-up" on the others by having the newsreader mark them as read. Next time you access that group, only new postings will be listed as unread.

For Tin users, the following list presents useful commands when reading messages:

Command	Purpose
Tab	Read next unread article in selected thread
Return	Read next unread article not in selected thread
q	Return to thread listing or return to newsgroup listing
c	Catch up on current group by marking all articles as read

Once you are familiar with your particular newsreader, reading messages is simple. It probably won't be long before you want to post a message with a question or a comment. Before explaining how to post, an etiquette lesson is in order.

Netiquette

As with any social community, USENET has some standards of conduct that participants in the community should respect. In this case, the etiquette of the USENET is known as netiquette. The fundamental rule of netiquette is to act toward your fellow USENETers with respect and courtesy; as Christians we have an even higher calling. Jesus himself set the standard in Matthew 19:19 when he said, "Love your neighbor as yourself." Although you may never physically meet your cyberspace "neighbor," the command remains the same.

By way of introduction, you should know that new users of USENET are known as newbies. Actually, *newbies* is a catch-all word that describes any new Internet users. Much like the word *freshman*, some negative connotations are associated. Fortunately, graduating beyond the newbie rank takes only a few weeks of surfing in cyberspace. With the Internet growing so fast, it doesn't take long to become more experienced than the thousands of people who came online a few days after you did.

Lurking

One practical way to learn how to love and respect other USENET users is to read a particular newsgroup for at least two weeks before posting. The habit of following a group without posting anything is known as lurking. While some online citizens complain about lurkers taking more than they give, lurking has its place. By doing this you will start to appreciate the particular culture that exists within a group. For instance, a **talk** group might react differently to a controversial issue than a **rec** group. The old saying applies here, "It is better to remain silent and appear as a fool than to open your mouth and remove all doubt." Know your audience.

Test Posting

Before participating in a discussion group it is wise to post a test message just to ensure that you've gotten the hang of USENET. Posting test messages is fine as long as you limit them to the **misc.test** newsgroup. It is annoying to browse **rec.music.christian** and see a dozen messages with the subject "Test, please ignore." When you post a message to **misc.test**, you should see it appear after a few hours. You'll also receive numerous confirmation notes telling you that your test message was received.

FAQs

New users all tend to ask the same questions. These popular inquiries are referred to as Frequently Asked Questions (FAQs). In response to such requests, most groups have assembled FAQ listings that contain these questions and their appropriate answers. These FAQ listings are posted to most newsgroups at least once a month and can also be found in the **news.answers** groups. Read the FAQ listing (if one exists) for a particular group before posting a question. Both you and your cyberspace companions will be happier.

Spamming

Thanks to an infamous post by a couple of lawyers, *spamming* has become a commonly used word in the USENET lexicon. To spam means to post the same message to numerous newsgroups, many of which have no relation to the subject of the note. The most notorious spamming incidents occur when someone posts the same message to every single USENET group. You haven't seen electronic wrath until you've witnessed a spamming backlash.

If you are selling a software product that permits Apple Macintosh and IBM PC–compatible computers to share files, it is reasonable to cross-post your message to `misc.forsale.computers.pc-clone` and `misc.forsale.computers.mac`. However, a message about church planting should not be posted in both `soc.religion.christian` and `rec.arts.movies`. Use common sense when cross-posting messages.

Flaming

Most folks who cruise USENET are friendly, helpful people who follow the rules of netiquette and contribute positively to the online community. However there are times, often in unmoderated groups, when things get heated and nasty. Since USENET is filled with virtually instant information when someone steps out of line, a number of people will immediately respond with sharp attacks aimed at the messenger. This type of attack message is called a flame. Flames are like family arguments—heated, often nasty, and generally without value. The best advice is to avoid them. If you really feel compelled to criticize someone, send them a polite note directly through e-mail.

You should be aware that some people intentionally post messages trying to start a flame war. As its name suggests, a flame war occurs when countless flame messages are posted to a particular group. This makes it more difficult to find useful information and generally clogs up a newsgroup for days. You can often tell that someone is trying to start a flame war when they post a message that is blatantly against the views of a particular group. A message encouraging people to listen to satanic music posted in `rec.music.christian` is probably a good example. Also, cross-posting messages to opposite groups (such as `alt.christnet` and `alt.atheist`) is usually a clue that someone is trying to bait readers.

Trolling

When someone posts a message that is intended to start a flame war or other vacuous discussion, it is called trolling. As previously mentioned, this can be done by posting something to an inappropriate group. More often, however, it is accomplished by posting a message that is clearly in error. For instance, suppose someone posts a message in a Christian group saying that God gave Moses the Ten Commandments on three stone tablets. Dozens of people will probably post a message pointing out that the commandments were written on two tablets. Though it could have been a genuine mistake, the original poster was probably trolling for a response. If the newsgroup gets flooded with messages correcting the so-called mistake, then the troll was successful. If a message appears to be a troll, the best thing to do is ignore it.

Additional Rules of the Road

What follows are a few rules of the road that will make your USENET experience more positive and hopefully prevent you from making a bad first impression.

- *Be sure that the subject of your post matches the message's content.* This is particularly valid if you are responding to a previous posting. It is not uncommon to pick up a discussion in the middle, based on an interesting subject line, only to realize that the participants have moved on to other topics. If the discussion strays from the original subject, then change the subject accordingly.

- *Be sure that the message is posted to the appropriate group.* Folks in a baseball discussion group really are not interested in hearing your views on the upcoming election. And unless the group is geared toward debate or controversial discussion, don't jump into a group that you disagree with and start attacking their views. A special caution to believers: Please don't visit other groups and start posting evangelistic messages like "You are going to hell if you don't accept Jesus." While you may be doctrinally correct, you are not loving the participants in the other group with this violation of netiquette. USENET can be a tremendous forum for witnessing, but do it in the proper context.

- *Limit postings to an appropriate geographical range.* For example, if you have a sofa for sale in Washington, D.C., there is no point in advertising it all over the world. Post the message in `dc.forsale` rather than `misc.forsale`.

- *If you post a question, remember to monitor the newsgroup to get your answer.* It's considered rude to ask a question and then state, "Please respond via e-mail since I do not follow this group." If you expect others to take the time to answer your question, the least you can do is take the time to look for it. Sometimes, of course, someone does post a message that lends itself to an e-mail response. A good example relates to the `misc.forsale` hierarchy. Suppose someone posts a message selling a stereo for two hundred dollars and you are interested. By all means, send an e-mail note directly to the seller. Millions of people are not interested in reading a message that displays your negotiating skills.

- *Don't include too much of an original message in a posted reply.* As with Internet e-mail, only include as much of the original message as you need to establish your point. A good rule of thumb is to make your response longer than what you include from the original post.

- *Limit the length of your signature block.* Signature blocks are helpful because they allow people to see who you are and how to reach you. Good USENETers will limit their signature blocks to four lines. It is frustrating to read a three-line message followed by a ten-line signature block.

- *Don't post chain letters or get-rich-quick schemes.* You will not only violate numerous usage regulations but also will incur the wrath of USENETers for many generations. Just don't do it.

By following these netiquette lessons you will make the USENET a friendlier and more useful place.

Posting Messages

After all of that, there isn't much to say about posting. Again, if you have never posted a message to USENET, start by posting a test message in the `misc.test` group. Remember that it may take a few hours or longer for your message to appear. Believe it or not, some things actually take time on the Internet! Once you see your test message, experiment with posting replies. Again, use `misc.test` for this. As soon as you are comfortable with posting to `misc.test`, have become familiar with the culture of the newsgroups, and have understood the rules of proper netiquette, post away!

Tin users should note that there are different posting commands used while reading a particular newsgroup. The list below should get you started:

Command	Purpose
w	Posts a message on a new topic
f	Posts a follow-up message in the current thread and includes some of the original message
F	Posts a follow-up message in the current thread but does *not* include the original message
r	Replies to the message's author through e-mail and includes some of the original message
R	Replies to the message's author through e-mail but does *not* include the original message

Be aware that in moderated groups your message could be discarded if it is not on topic or violates other community rules of the newsgroup. If a message doesn't appear for a few days, and you don't think that it was deleted by a moderator, feel free to repost it. It is uncommon for news systems to lose messages, but it does happen.

USENET posting isn't really that different from posting a message on a BBS or commercial online forum, but since the audience is significantly larger, you will find USENET an invaluable resource.

USENET Shorthand

USENET world has its own jargon. For instance, you may find a reference to snail-mail. This refers to mail sent through the U.S. Postal System rather than electronically. (You can probably discern the implication.) More commonly you will notice that people often use acronyms to shorten commonly used phrases. While most people know that FYI in a business memo means "For Your Information," few know that ROTFL in a USENET posting means "Rolling on the Floor Laughing." There are a number of staple acronyms found on USENET and in e-mail messages. Here is a primer list:

Acronym	Translation
BTW	By The Way
CC	Carbon Copy
FAQ	Frequently Asked Question (can refer to a FAQ listing for a group)
FWIW	For What It's Worth
FYI	For Your Information
IMHO	In My Humble Opinion
IMNSHO	In My Not So Humble Opinion
IOW	In Other Words
OTOH	On The Other Hand

RE	Regarding
ROTFL	Rolling On The Floor Laughing
RSN	Real Soon Now (As in, "the new release will be ready RSN")
RTFM	A crass way to tell someone to Read The Manual. Not a good way to love your online neighbor.
TANSTAAFL	There Ain't No Such Thing As A Free Lunch
TIA	Thanks In Advance
TTFN	Ta-Ta For Now
WRT	With Respect To
YMMV	Your Mileage May Vary (You may get different results)

Newsgroups for Beginners

Besides `misc.test`, there are a number of newsgroups that USENET beginners will find particularly helpful. One of these is `news.answers`, which was mentioned in the Netiquette section under FAQs. The FAQ lists for the different newsgroups are posted to `news.answers` on a regular basis, so by monitoring it you will quickly become familiar with USENET. Some of the more voluminous regular posts include a list of all active USENET groups, a list of the USENET moderators, and even a series of lists describing publicly accessible mailing lists. Another group worth monitoring is `news.announce.newusers`. This newsgroup contains periodic postings of interest to new USENET users. `News.newusers.questions` is a catch-all group that encourages newbies to post questions. No relevant question is off-limits, so this is a good group to follow until you become fluent with USENET.

Christian Newsgroups

There are a number of Christian USENET groups that are also worth exploring. Two of the classics, mentioned previously, are `soc.religion.christian` and `rec.music.christian`. `Soc.religion.christian` is a moderated group intended for general discussions about the Christian faith, theology, and practical Christianity. Historically, the moderator has done an admirable job wading through denominational differences and divisive issues. It is a high-quality newsgroup that can be a good resource as well as an encouragement. `Rec.music.christian` is an unmoderated group that caters to those interested in Christian music, particularly contemporary music and musicians. It is an excellent source of industry news and reviews of the latest releases. Due to the lack of moderation, the group can sometimes get bogged down in repetitive discussions about the pros and cons of a particular Christian artist. Nevertheless, it is generally a good read.

During the past year Christians have taken a more active role on USENET and have set up a number of new groups. You will find different strengths and weaknesses within the various groups. Unmoderated ones can become particularly unruly when a troublemaker decides to post an obscene or deliberately offensive message. The best strategy is to monitor a number of groups for a while and then subscribe to the ones that you find useful.

Additional Christian USENET groups can be found in the Christian Internet Directory (appendix C).

10

Telnet

How would you like to be able to browse the Library of Congress card catalog from your desk? Maybe a look at the weather around the world would excite you. How about logging in to your computer in Washington, D.C., while you are on a business trip in Washington State? All of these scenarios, and many more, are made possible with the Internet service called Telnet.

What Is Telnet?

Typically, when you connect to an online service you place a phone call using your modem. Once you have logged in to the online service, Telnet provides you the opportunity to connect to other computers attached to the Internet. Essentially, Telnet places an "Internet phone call" between your host computer and a separate remote computer *without* actually using a modem. Once you connect to the remote computer, it looks just as if your modem had actually called that system. Here's an example:

```
explorer:[/opt2/usr/g-rhie] telnet iclnet93.iclnet.org
Trying 199.2.101.10 ...
Connected to iclnet93.iclnet.org.
Escape character is '^]'.

To access ICLnet BBS/Internet type 'guest' (no quotes) if you
are a new user or type your registered Login Name (ie joe43).
```

```
Current Node: (iclnet93)
login: g-rhie
Password:

Welcome to the . . .

      IIIIII  CCCCc   LL
        II    cCC CCC  LL                                 tt
        II    CC    Cc LL                                 tt
        II    CC       LL                                 tttttttt
        II    CC       LL       nn nnnn    eeee    tt
        II    CC       LL       nnN nn    ee  ee   tt
        II    CC       LL       nn   nn   eeeeeeee tt
        II    CC    Cc LL       nn   nn   ee       tt
        II    cCC CCC  LLLLLLL  nn   nn   ee  ee   tt  tt
      IIIIII  CCCCc    LLLLLLL  nn   nn    eeeee      tttt

              BULLETIN BOARD AND INFORMATION SYSTEM

     For the Christian Higher Education & Professional Community

   Phone:(503)598-7889 Fax:(503)598-8571 Modem Dialup:(503)598-7884
                    IP Address: 199.2.101.10

   << Using the FreePort BBS Software created by Case Western
   Reserve Univ. >>

   Press Enter/Return to continue:
```

Did you notice that when we connected to the remote computer, we were prompted to enter our username and password? This is because we actually logged in to the computer just as if an actual phone call had been placed. This means, of course, that you can only Telnet to computers on which you have accounts. Fortunately, some organizations have established publicly accessible systems that anyone can access with Telnet. These computers often contain library information or other tools for the online visitor.

Take note of the statement in the previous example that said: Escape character is '^]'. This tells you how to exit the Telnet session if it freezes. Recall that the ^ key often refers to the Control key on your keyboard. Thus, you can escape out of this Telnet session by typing the Control key and the right square bracket (]) at the same time.

Once you make a Telnet connection, you can then move around freely in the remote system. The Telnet connection will become transparent.

Making a Telnet Connection

Opening a Telnet session requires that you first know the address of the computer to which you want to connect. These addresses conform to the **network.organization.type** format that was discussed in the Electronic Mail chapter (chapter 8). That is, you need to know the address information typically found on the right side of the @ sign in an e-mail address. For example, to open a Telnet connection to the Library of Congress from a UNIX shell, you would type:

telnet locis.loc.gov

Certain online services make connections even easier by offering Telnet as a menu choice. After selecting the Telnet menu option, enter the appropriate address (in this case **locis.loc.gov**) to complete the connection.

Once you have connected to a remote site, you may be asked for a username and/or password, much like when you log in to a local system. If this occurs you'll need to provide the appropriate information for the remote computer. Note that you should not enter the username and password that you use for your local online service, since they will not be recognized by the remote system. Often publicly accessible sites omit the username and/or password prompts altogether, proceeding directly to an options menu.

The example below shows a Telnet connection to the Library of Congress. Since it is a publicly accessible site, a username or password is not needed to gain access.

```
explorer:[/opt2/usr/g-rhie] telnet locis.loc.gov
Trying 140.147.254.3 . . .
Connected to locis.loc.gov.
Escape character is '^]'.

     L O C I S : LIBRARY OF CONGRESS INFORMATION SYSTEM

     To make a choice: type a number, then press ENTER

1    Library of Congress Catalog        4    Braille and Audio

2    Federal Legislation                5    Organizations

3    Copyright Information              6    Foreign Law

*    *    *    *    *    *    *    *    *    *
7    Searching Hours and Basics
```

```
 8   Documentation and Classes
 9   Library of Congress General Information
10   Library of Congress Fast Facts
11   * * Announcements * *

12   Comments and Logoff

Choice: 1
```

As you can see, Telnet is fairly straightforward. Most publicly accessible sites have a menu system that makes it easy for you to move around once you have connected. In the unlikely chance that the system lacks a menu, you can navigate using the standard UNIX commands that are listed in chapter 5.

Hytelnet

To further assist users, a specialized version of Telnet was developed called Hytelnet. Hytelnet is a menu-based Telnet system that allows you to open a Telnet connection by selecting a desired location from a menu. This means you do not have to remember any Internet addresses or log-in information. You start the service simply by typing **hytelnet**. This will bring you to a main menu. As you move through the menu hierarchy, there will be lists of existing public Telnet sites along with descriptions of what can be found at each. With your cursor on or beside a menu item, simply press the Return key and Hytelnet will automatically execute the appropriate Telnet command and enter the username/password combination necessary for that system. Hytelnet makes the Telnet process truly painless.

Shown below is an example of the Hytelnet service. Take note of the easy-to-read menu.

```
Welcome to HYTELNET version 6.7
        May 14, 1994

What is HYTELNET?          <WHATIS>
Library catalogs           <SITES1>
Other resources            <SITES2>
Help files for catalogs    <OP000>
Catalog interfaces         <SYS000>
Internet Glossary          <GLOSSARY>
Telnet tips                <TELNET>
Telnet/TN3270 escape keys  <ESCAPE.KEY>
Key-stroke commands        <HELP>
```

```
..............................................................
Up/Down arrows MOVE    Left/Right arrows SELECT     ? for HELP anytime

   m returns here      i searches the index           q quits
..............................................................

            HYTELNET 6.7 was written by Peter Scott
            E-mail address: aa375@freenet.carleton.ca
               Unix and VMS software by Earl Fogel
```

Where to Begin

If you are interested in using the Internet for research, you will find a number of college library systems online. The following chart lists some libraries (both Christian and secular) that are available using Telnet.

Address	Username	Library
alcon.acu.edu	alcpac	Abilene Library Consortium (Abilene Christian University)
libopac.caltech.edu	library	California Institute of Technology
host.clic.edu	cpac	Concordia College
hollis.harvard.edu	hollis	Harvard University
mcis.messiah.edu	opac	Messiah College
locis.loc.gov	(Not needed)	Library of Congress
jerome.spu.edu	pac	Seattle Pacific University
lib.swbts.edu	public	Southwest Baptist Theological Seminary

Although libraries are the most common public Telnet resource, there are a few Telnet sites that specifically pertain to Christians:

Address	Username	Description
iclnet93.iclnet.org	(Follow prompts)	Institute for Christian Leadership bulletin board. Established for Christians involved in higher education as faculty, staff, or administrators.
rf1.cuis.edu	luthernet	Lutheran Church-Missouri Synod network for congregations and other denominational affiliates.

And finally, you can get the latest weather forecast by Telnetting to **hermes.merit.edu** and logging in as **um-weather**.

11

File Transfer Protocol

Imagine, if you will, grabbing an armload of books from your bookshelves, putting them on a special shelf in your garage, and then leaving the garage door unlocked so that anyone could enter and borrow at their leisure. Further imagine hundreds of thousands of people doing the same thing. You could go from neighborhood to neighborhood and browse hardbacks to your heart's content. It would be like having libraries on practically every street.

Essentially, this is what people do on the Internet. Folks take various software packages, articles, pictures, and other goodies and put them somewhere on their computer so that others can have access. From electronic Bibles to games, there are more files accessible on the Internet than books at your local library. To access these, you must connect to a computer that stores the files that you want and then tell your computer to copy the files from that remote site. Once you get the files, you do not have to return them; they are yours to keep. The Internet service that enables you to do this is called File Transfer Protocol.

FTP

FTP is a cousin to Telnet. Recall that Telnet allows you to connect to a remote computer on the Internet and perform tasks, just as if you were locally connected. Similarly, FTP allows you to log into a remote computer but solely for the purpose of transferring files.

Depending on your system, you initiate an FTP session either by selecting FTP from a menu, or by typing **ftp** followed by the Internet address of the location to which you are going. For instance, if you wanted to open an FTP connection to Washington University in St. Louis (which, by the way, is a popular site to find files), you would execute the following UNIX command:

```
ftp wuarchive.wustl.edu
```

You would then follow the prompts and enter your username and appropriate password.

You are probably wondering how you can successfully log on to a remote site when no one's ever provided you with a username/password combination appropriate for that system. Excellent question. Fortunately there is a special type of FTP, known as anonymous FTP, that has been adopted to resolve this dilemma.

Anonymous FTP

Anonymous FTP permits you to log in to a computer using **anonymous** as your username and your Internet e-mail address as your password. Once logged on you can peruse a special array of directories and files to download at your leisure. Furthering the library analogy, recall that there are two types of people who access the books in the garage: the residents of that particular house, and the visitors who come in through the garage. If you have an account on the computer to which you are FTPing, you are like the residents of the house. You can look at the books in the garage, but you're also free to unlock the door to the house and examine everything inside. Visitors to the home are permitted to enter the garage and borrow from a subset of the homeowner's library, but cannot enter the main residence. Anonymous FTP is similar—people can access files specially earmarked for visitors but cannot roam around the entire computer system. Some anonymous FTP sites also allow visitors to upload files, so others, too, may get copies.

Whenever you connect to an anonymous FTP site, you are taxing computer resources. If multiple anonymous users are downloading files, the host computer will not be able to perform daily functions quickly. Since organizations generously offer anonymous FTP sites to service the Internet community, try to return the consideration by restricting your FTP connections to non-business hours.

Directory Structure

The FTP file system is broken down by directories, which act as hierarchical drawers in a file cabinet. Note that UNIX directories use a forward slash (/) to separate subdirectories. Thus in the case of the **/pub/windows/games** directory, **games** is a subdirectory of **windows**, which is a subdirectory of **pub**, which is a subdirectory of the /, or root, directory. A typical directory tree might look like this:

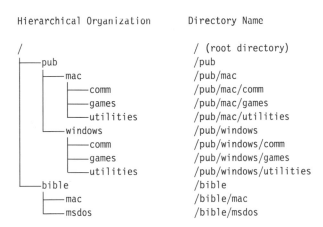

```
Hierarchical Organization       Directory Name

/                               / (root directory)
├──pub                          /pub
│   ├──mac                      /pub/mac
│   │   ├──comm                 /pub/mac/comm
│   │   ├──games                /pub/mac/games
│   │   └──utilities            /pub/mac/utilities
│   └──windows                  /pub/windows
│       ├──comm                 /pub/windows/comm
│       ├──games                /pub/windows/games
│       └──utilities            /pub/windows/utilities
└──bible                        /bible
    ├──mac                      /bible/mac
    └──msdos                    /bible/msdos
```

FTP Commands

Once you have FTPed to a given location and logged in with your username (in this case, **anonymous**) and password (your Internet address), then you are ready to move around the system. The following UNIX commands allow you to navigate through an FTP site. (Some of these were introduced in chapter 5). As always, italicized words indicate parameters that you must fill in when issuing the command.

Command	Function
ascii	Sets transfer mode required for text files
binary	Sets transfer mode required for non-text (binary) files
cd *name*	Changes to the directory **name**, which must be a subdirectory of the current directory
cd */name1/name2*	Changes to the directory **/name1/name2**
cd ..	Backs up one directory level
cd /	Backs up to the top-level directory
dir	Lists files in the current directory
get *filename*	Retrieves the file **filename** from a remote computer. Remember that you need to execute the **ascii** or **binary** command prior to getting a file.

get *file* |more	Allows you to read the contents of the text file *file* without exiting FTP.
help	Activates the online help system. It will show you a list of the FTP commands available. More detailed assistance is available by typing **help *command*** where command is a particular command in question (e.g. **help mget**).
ls	Lists files in the current directory
ls -l	Lists files and their sizes (in bytes)
|more	Pauses a listing at the end of every screen rather than scrolling continuously. Used in conjunction with other commands such as **ls** and **cat**. For example, **ls |more** will list files, pausing the list after every screen. To continue, press the space bar.
mget *file1 file2*	Retrieves multiple files at one time. In this case you would retrieve the programs called *file1* and *file2*.
quit	Terminates an FTP connection

Sample FTP Sessions

Shown below is a sample FTP session, similar to what you might encounter if you were browsing for available files at the remote site **wiretap.spies.com**. Pay special attention to the boldface commands.

```
explorer:[/opt2/usr/dkennedy] ftp wiretap.spies.com
Connected to wiretap.spies.com.
220 wiretap.spies.com FTP server (Version wu-2.4(5) Sat Oct 1 15:52:02 PDT
1994)ready.
Name (wiretap.spies.com:dkennedy): anonymous
331 Guest login ok, send your complete e-mail address as password.
Password:
230-
230-wiretap.spies.com
230-
230-Welcome to the Internet Wiretap FTP server.
230-
230 Guest login ok, access restrictions apply.
ftp> ls
200 PORT command successful.
150 Opening ASCII mode data connection for file list.
Library
Books
Etext
226 Transfer complete.
143 bytes received in 0.0067 seconds (21 Kbytes/s)
ftp> cd Library
250 CWD command successful.
ftp> ls
200 PORT command successful.
150 Opening ASCII mode data connection for file list.
Classic
Zines
```

```
Music
README
Religion
226 Transfer complete.
141 bytes received in 0.0056 seconds (25 Kbytes/s)
ftp> cd Religion
250 CWD command successful.
ftp> ls
200 PORT command successful.
150 Opening ASCII mode data connection for file list.
README
Anglican
Catholic
Creeds
226 Transfer complete.
111 bytes received in 0.0041 seconds (26 Kbytes/s)
ftp> cd Creeds
250 CWD command successful.
ftp> ls
200 PORT command successful.
150 Opening ASCII mode data connection for file list.
apostles.zip
nicene.txt
226 Transfer complete.
19 bytes received in 0.04 seconds (0.46 Kbytes/s)
ftp>
```

Now let's watch the user retrieve the file **apostles.zip**. As you will learn, the **.zip** extension denotes that the file is compressed. Therefore, since it is not a text file, the **binary** command must be entered before retrieving it.

```
ftp> binary
200 Type set to I.
ftp> get apostles.zip
200 PORT command successful.
150 Opening Binary mode data connection for apostles.zip (8049 bytes)
226 Transfer complete.
local: apostles.zip remote: apostles.zip
8049 bytes received in .44 seconds (18 Kbytes/s)
ftp> quit
221 Goodbye.
explorer:[/opt2/usr/dkennedy]
```

Downloading Files

In most cases, FTP is only half of the file transfer story. When you retrieve a file from an FTP site, it is loaded onto your UNIX account or host computer. Moving the file off your host computer and onto your personal computer is called downloading. The specifics of this process vary somewhat based on your terminal emulation software. Nevertheless, there are some fundamentals to consider.

Like most other communications issues, there are a variety of protocols used for transferring files. The four main transfer protocols are Xmodem, Ymodem, Zmodem, and Kermit. Although the technical specifications of each differ, all can be used to download both text and binary files. Which protocol you use will often depend on what your communications software can support. Zmodem is the protocol of choice as it allows you to transfer multiple files with a single command and is typically the fastest. If your communications software cannot support Zmodem, you should choose Ymodem or Xmodem. While being the most common, Kermit is also the slowest of the protocols and should only be used if no other options are available.

In order to download software, you must tell the host computer to send the file and your personal computer to receive it. The first part is often done by selecting the download option off a menu. If you are using a standard UNIX shell, you will need one of the following commands:

Command	Protocol
sz *filename*	Zmodem
sz -a *filename*	Zmodem text transfer
sb *filename*	Ymodem
sb -a *filename*	Ymodem text transfer
sx *filename*	Xmodem
sx -a *filename*	Xmodem text transfer
kermit	Kermit (type help at the kermit> prompt for more commands)

The following examples use the Xmodem and Zmodem protocols to demonstrate how the host computer can be instructed to transfer the file **apostles.zip**. Note that only one of these commands is necessary two are shown simply for comparison.

```
explorer:[/opt2/usr/dkennedy] sx apostles.zip
Sending apostles.zip, 63 XMODEM blocks. Start your local XMODEM receive

(Issue Xmodem receive command from communications software)

explorer:[/opt2/usr/dkennedy]

explorer:[/opt2/usr/dkennedy] sz apostles.zip
```

```
*B00000000000000

(Issue Zmodem receive command from communications software)

explorer:[/opt2/usr/dkennedy]
```

Once you issue the UNIX command, the host system waits to get a signal from your communications software to begin the transfer. This signal cannot come, however, until your personal computer knows how it should receive the incoming file. From within your communications software you must first select the option that says "download file" (or some similar wording). The software will then prompt you for the transfer protocol (e.g. Xmodem) and where, on your computer, to save the file (e.g. drive C). Once this is done the transfer will commence. Most communications software will tell you the estimated transfer time and what percentage of the transfer has been completed, as seen in figure 14.

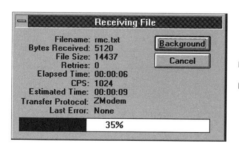

Figure 14

File Transfer Status

NcFTP

Some Internet providers may offer an easier alternative to FTP called NcFTP. Essentially it is a version of the FTP service designed for new users who are exclusively using anonymous FTP. NcFTP is run by typing **ncftp** followed by the Internet address of a specific site. Thus, if you want to make a NcFTP connection to **ftp.cica.indiana.edu** you would issue the following command:

```
ncftp ftp.cica.indiana.edu
```

The NcFTP product automatically logs you in anonymously so you don't have to mess with the username and password prompts. Furthermore, it allows you to view text files online without having to issue the **get file**

|more command. If you have NcFTP available, you may want to consider using it as your primary FTP service.

Graphical FTP

In addition to the text-based UNIX FTP command, there are a number of graphical FTP interfaces available. America Online's Internet Connection area contains a user-friendly FTP system that will even automatically perform an anonymous FTP login. Proprietary Internet interfaces, including PSI's Pipeline and Netcom's NetCruiser, sport point-and-click FTP front ends that eliminate the need for any of the UNIX commands. For those who connect to the Internet using SLIP/PPP connections, there are some shareware FTP programs that also simplify the file transfer process. WS-FTP for Windows and Fetch for the Mac are examples of such applications. An FTP session using Fetch is shown below.

Figure 15

FTP
Using Fetch

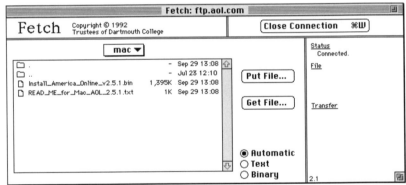

You can download these programs from the following anonymous FTP sites:

Program	Platform	Address	Directory	File
Fetch	Mac	ftp.iquest.com	/pub/mac/tcp	fetch*.*
WS-FTP	Windows	ftp.cica.indiana.edu	/pub/pc/win3/winsock	ws_ftp*.*

Finding Files to FTP

The catch with FTP is that it is often harder to find where the information is located than it is to actually acquire the information. Fortunately, there are a few ways to find where specific files are residing. One method is to ask other users. While you are welcome to post a message on a relevant news-group asking for pointers to information, be sure to first read that news-group's FAQ list. Many FAQs provide the Internet addresses of relevant anonymous FTP sites. Other ways to locate files include Archie and the World Wide Web.

Archie

Archie is a database that contains the locations of millions of files found at various FTP sites. Although not every anonymous FTP site participates in the Archie network, it is regularly updated. If your Internet provider offers the Archie service, you can begin by typing **archie**. This will activate a list of options that can be used when doing an Archie search.

```
explorer:[/opt2/usr/beverett] archie
Usage: archie [-acelorstvLV] [-m hits] [-N level] string
          -a : list matches as Alex filenames
          -c : case sensitive substring search
          -e : exact string match (default)
          -r : regular expression search
          -s : case insensitive substring search
          -l : list one match per line
          -t : sort inverted by date
     -m hits : specifies maximum number of hits to return (default 95)
 -o filename : specifies file to store results in
     -h host : specifies server host
          -L : list known servers and current default
    -N level : specifies query niceness level (0-35765)
explorer:[/opt2/usr/beverett]
```

Based on the key words that you indicate, Archie will search its database and tell you what files match your request. The example below shows a subset of the search results on the word *Christian*.

```
explorer:[/opt2/usr/beverett] archie -s christian

Host julian.uwo.ca

    Location: /doc/FAQ/music
       DIRECTORY drwxr-xr-x   512   Jul 16 23:30 christian

Host cs.bu.edu

    Location: /CN/keywords
```

```
             FILE -rw-r-r-    1029    Jun 4 1993 christian

Host rtfm.mit.edu

    Location: /pub/usenet-by-group/news.answers/music
       DIRECTORY drwxrwxr-x   512   Sep 5 19:11 christian
    Location: /pub/usenet-by-group/rec.answers/music
       DIRECTORY drwxrwxr-x   512   Sep 5 19:11 christian
    Location: /pub/usenet-by-hierarchy/news/answers/music
       DIRECTORY drwxrwxr-x   512   Sep 5 19:11 christian
    Location: /pub/usenet-by-hierarchy/rec/answers/music
       DIRECTORY drwxrwxr-x   512   Sep 5 19:11 christian
    Location: /pub/usenet-by-hierarchy/rec/music
       DIRECTORY drwxrwxr-x   512   Oct 18 02:20 christian
    Location: /pub/usenet-by-hierarchy/soc/religion
       DIRECTORY drwxrwxr-x   512   Aug 14 15:49 christian

Host grasp.insa-lyon.fr

    Location: /pub/faq-by-newsgroup/rec/rec.music.info/music
       DIRECTORY drwxrwxr-x   512   Sep 19 11:52 christian
    Location: /pub/faq/music
       DIRECTORY drwxrwxr-x   512   Sep 19 11:52 christian

Host unix.hensa.ac.uk

    Location: /pub/uunet/usenet/news.answers/music
       DIRECTORY drwxr-xr-x   512   Sep 19 11:57 christian
explorer:[/opt2/usr/beverett]
```

If you do not have access to a local Archie program, you may access a public Archie client using Telnet. The following table shows the addresses of some Archie clients available via Telnet:

Address	Location
archie.ans.net	New York
archie.rutgers.edu	New Jersey
archie.sura.net	Maryland
archie.unl.edu	Nebraska

By Telnetting to one of these addresses and logging in with the username **archie**, you will be able to perform your search. After you log in, type **help** to receive usage instructions. Since these sites receive heavy usage, try to access the one closest to you geographically.

As a last resort, you can send Archie commands through Internet e-mail. Send a mail message to **archie@archie.sura.net** with the single word **help** in the body of the message. You will then receive further instructions on how to perform your searches through e-mail.

World Wide Web

Another way to locate files is by using the World Wide Web. Many Web pages have pointers to files that you can download simply by clicking on them. As with other material on the Internet, there is no official organization to the Web; however, a good place to begin your software search is by visiting the Yahoo server. Point your Web browser to **http://www.yahoo.com** to view an extensive subject directory of the WWW. If you perform a search on the keyword *software* you will find pointers to numerous Web pages, many of which have downloadable files.

Other Software Issues

File Compression

From the end-user's perspective, files obtained from an anonymous FTP site are free. Remember, however, that someone has to purchase the hard drives and modems required to support an FTP site. In an effort to reduce storage and transmission costs, file compression techniques were developed.

Since many files found on the Internet are compressed, you will need to be able to decompress them before they can be used. A decompression utility will perform this task for you. You can usually find, and download, decompression programs from your online service or an anonymous FTP site.

Because there are a variety of decompression programs available, it is important to first determine what type of compression was used on your file. Compression types can be easily identified by the extension attached to the filename in question. For instance, compressed UNIX files often end in **.Z** or **.gz**, while compressed files for IBM-compatibles usually end in **.zip** or **.arc**. Many compressed Macintosh files have two extensions. The **.sit** extension (which denotes the compression type) is often followed by the **.hqx** extension (which identifies a special BinHex treatment performed to preserve certain Macintosh attributes in the file).

Shown below is a table that lists anonymous FTP sites from which decompression programs can be downloaded. Before you FTP any of these files, check with your Internet provider to see if the file is available locally. Due to constant updating, exact file names are not included here. Instead, part of the file name has been listed with an asterisk to indicate that there are probably other characters in the title. For instance, **pkz*.exe** might actually represent a file called **pkz204g.exe**.

Extension	Platform	FTP Location	Directory	Filename
.arc	IBM	wuarchive.wustl.edu	/systems/ibmpc/simtel/arc/	pk*.exe
.bin	Mac	mac.archive.umich.edu	/mac/util/compression/	stuffitlite*.sea.hqx
.cpt	Mac	mac.archive.umich.edu	/mac/util/compression/	stuffitlite*.sea.hqx
.hqx	Mac	mac.archive.umich.edu	/mac/util/compression/	stuffitlite*.sea.hqx
.sit	Mac	mac.archive.umich.edu	/mac/util/compression/	stuffitlite*.sea.hqx
.Z	UNIX	oak.oakland.edu	/pub/misc/unix/	compress*.tar.Z
.zip	IBM	pogue.admin.lsa.umich.edu	/msdos/compression/zip/	pkz*.exe
.zip	Mac	mac.archive.umich.edu	/mac/util/compression/	unzip*.cpt.hqx
.zoo	IBM	ftp.cso.uiuc.edu	/systems/ibmpc/simtel/zoo/	zoo*.exe
.zoo	Mac	mac.archive.umich.edu	/mac/util/compression/	maczoo*.cpt.hqx
.zoo	UNIX	oak.oakland.edu	/pub/misc/unix/	zoo*.tar.Z

Shareware

If you have ever purchased expensive and nonreturnable computer software only to be disappointed that it didn't live up to your expectations, you will be delighted with the multitude of software available from anonymous FTP sites. Although you won't find commercial software on an anonymous FTP site, there are thousands upon thousands of useful products available for downloading. Generally, these are either public domain or shareware software.

Public-domain products make no promises regarding accuracy, capabilities, or support. They are considered noncopyrighted material and may be freely distributed, and even modified, by users. These products are similar to books, like the King James Bible, whose copyright has expired.

Shareware was developed based on a "try before you buy" philosophy. Shareware software has been copyrighted by the author(s) but placed on the Internet for interested users to download and try. Sometimes the versions are incomplete or crippled; other times the software will expire and lock up after a fixed number of days. Sometimes, though, the software is complete and fully functional. If you like the product and plan to continue to use it, you are instructed to send a specified dollar amount to the author to purchase a license for its use. The author may then send you a manual or more complete version of the program. Other times you will simply receive a note saying that you are now a registered user.

Ideally, shareware is a win-win situation for both the author and user. The software author gets wide distribution of a product for minimal marketing investment, while the user gets the opportunity to test-drive software before making a purchase. Don't let the concept fool you into believing that all shareware is inferior to its commercial counterparts. Many shareware products are as good or superior to the commercial stuff. Unfortunately, most users who download shareware continue to use it past the evaluation period without paying for it. Please, if you download a shareware product that you elect to keep, register the package with the author. If you find the product not to your liking, then simply delete it. Shareware is a unique concept that can really benefit the cyberspace community. It would be regrettable if the concept died because the registration requirement was so often disregarded by users.

Viruses

While many FTP sites and bulletin board systems screen programs before making them available for download, there is still the chance that a program could have a virus. A computer virus is exactly what it sounds like, a contaminant that causes harm to your computer. Viruses range from amusing (such as putting a smiley face on your screen) to devastatingly destructive (like erasing everything off your hard drive). Viruses don't just happen; they are created by computer wizards who are either prankish or cruel. Since viruses can cause irreparable damage to your system, it is important to take precautions.

First, back up your hard drive regularly. While this won't prevent a virus from hurting your system, it will make it possible to recover from a problem. Second, ensure that you have a virus-scanning program on your computer that regularly checks the memory and files for viruses. There are a number of virus scanners commercially available or found on anonymous FTP sites. Scan every program you download to ensure that it is virus-free. Although the overwhelming majority of files are perfectly fine, it is far better to be safe than sorry.

Places to Start

Since numerous anonymous FTP sites exist and many have overlapping content, you may want to explore various locations before settling on your favorite systems. Note that most anonymous FTP sites store information in either the **/pub** directory or a subdirectory of **/pub**. Here are some sites to get you started:

Address	*Content*
`bible.acu.edu`	Missionary, cell-church, and exegetical resources
`ftp.cica.indiana.edu`	Various Windows-related files
`ftp.spss.com`	Bible study information including software and commentaries
`iclnet93.iclnet.org`	Christian Research Institute, Focus on the Family, and Taize Community materials
`kuyper.cs.pitt.edu`	Various Christian writings including those of Augustine and Chesterton
`mac.archive.umich.edu`	Various Macintosh files
`wuarchive.wustl.edu`	Various files for IBM-compatible and Macintosh computers

12

Gopher

Despite the wealth of information available on the Internet, many people are put off by the complexity of navigation. Gopher is one of a number of second-generation Internet tools that attempt to simplify things for the hesitant user.

What Is Gopher?

Gopher allows you to explore the Internet through topical menu systems called servers. Gopher servers, sometimes called "Gopher holes," have been developed at specific Internet sites and are thus organized geographically. Since the various Gopher servers interconnect with each other, you can often start at a particular location and move through Gopherspace based on topics rather than locations. What really makes Gopher popular is that it uses plain English.

The table that follows shows a few branches of the Gopher hierarchy.

```
Other Gopher and Information Servers
      ├─────Africa
      ├─────Europe
      │        └─United Kingdom
      │              └─Durham University
      └─────North America
               ├─Canada
               │     └─University of Toronto
               └─USA
                     ├─Illinois
                     │     ├─Concordia University
                     │     └─University of Illinois at Chicago
                     └─Michigan
                           ├─Calvin College
                           └─University of Michigan Libraries
```

Notice that the top level of the hierarchy is organized by continent, and the branches are organized by country, then by state, then by location name.

Essentially, when an Internet site wants to maintain a Gopher server, it will create its own Gopher server menu. Within this menu are subgroups that contain text files for viewing or additional menus. Gopher servers can, and usually do, include pointers to other Gopher servers. This means that menus at one server can actually contain information located at another Internet site. Users can select a title from the menu and then Gopher will "go for" the information, automatically connecting to another site. A Gopher menu can even launch a Telnet session. Since no complicated Internet addresses are necessary, you are free to focus on information rather than procedures.

Running Gopher

Like other Internet services, Gopher can be run in a number of ways. If your online provider uses a menu system, simply choose Gopher from that menu. UNIX shell accounts require that you type **gopher** at the command line and hit Return. If you are using Mosaic, you'll need to point to the Universal Resource Locator of the Gopher site in which you are interested (see chapter 13). When you run Gopher, you will automatically be connected to your local Gopher server. If your location doesn't have a Gopher server set up, you will probably be connected to the menu at the University of Minnesota, where Gopher was originally developed. If you don't have local access to Gopher, you can still take advantage of the Gopher features by using Telnet. The following table lists Gopher clients that you can reach via Telnet.

Address	Username
consultant.micro.umn.edu	gopher
gopher.msu.edu	gopher
panda.uiowa.edu	panda
ux1.cso.uiuc.edu	gopher

If you Telnet to one of these addresses and log in with the appropriate username, you will be connected to a publicly accessible Gopher server.

Navigating Gopher

Although the interfaces may differ, Gopher's fundamental menu structure remains the same. Let's examine a few common interfaces.

UNIX

```
                 Internet Gopher Information Client 2.0 p110

                   Root gopher server: gopher.wheaton.edu

-->   1.  Wheaton College Gopher Information and Help.
      2.  WHEATON COLLEGE...........Wheaton College Information/
      3.  GOPHERSPACE..................Gophers around the World/
      4.  VERONICA..............Keyword searches of gopherspace/
      5.  LIBRARIES..........................Library Catalogs/
      6.  RESEARCH.........................Study and Research/
      7.  NEWS..................................Issues and News/
      8.  INTERNET................Internet Related Information/
      9.  CHURCH.................Christian Studies Information/
      10. COMMUNITY....................Community Information/
      11. Automated Suggestion Form.
      12. SEARCH Wheaton's Gopher.



Press ? for Help, q to Quit                          Page: 1/1
```

As you can see, a Gopher server is essentially a topical menu. Menu choices will lead to either additional menus or text-based files. In UNIX, menu items often end with a slash, denoting an additional menu level, or with a period, denoting a document.

You can navigate the existing menu using the up and down arrow keys, or by typing the number of the selection you want. Once you have moved the pointer to your selection, you can move downstream, so to speak, by hitting Return or pressing the right arrow key. The left arrow key or **u**, for up, moves you back upstream to the previous menu that you were viewing. Finally, **q** quits Gopher.

Rather than traveling through the menus, you can directly connect to a Gopher server if you know its Internet address. This is accomplished with the following command:

```
gopher gopher.domainname
```

Just substitute the Internet address of your desired location in place of **domainname**. For example, if you want to connect to St. Olaf College and you know that its Internet Gopher address is **gopher.stolaf.edu**, then you would type:

```
gopher gopher.stolaf.edu
```

The system would automatically connect to the St. Olaf College Gopher server. Although not every Gopher server adheres to the **gopher.domain-name** convention, it is the most common.

Commercial Online Services

As with other Internet tools, commercial online services offer their own implementation of the Gopher interface. Shown in figure 16 is America Online's Gopher server.

Notice how America Online has already organized your choices into major subject headings. Folder icons are used to describe menu options while paper icons identify documents. As with everything on America Online, you navigate the Gopher server by using your mouse to double-click on the choice that you want to view. Once you choose a particular topic, AOL will present a selection of Gopher servers that match that topic. Be aware that you do have an option to view additional servers. By only showing you a subset, AOL achieves faster response time. Other commercial online services that support Gopher function similarly.

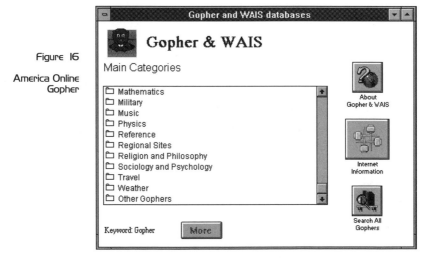

Figure 16

America Online Gopher

Reprinted with permission from America Online, Inc. All rights reserved.

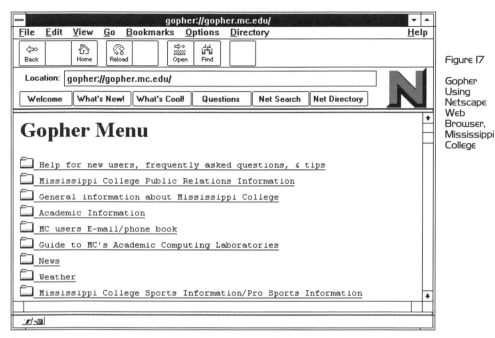

Figure 17

Gopher Using Netscape Web Browser, Mississippi College

Netscape Communications, Netscape, and Netscape Navigator are trademarks or registered trademarks of Netscape Communications Corporation.

Mosaic

Mosaic is a graphical front-end for the WWW which can be used with SLIP or PPP connections, which can also view Gopher sites. As with America Online, folder and paper icons are used to distinguish menu items. Mosaic users can navigate through Gopher using the mouse to click on the desired choices. Notice that the address of the current Gopher server is shown, in URL format, at the top of the screen.

Gopher Exploration

Because Gopher is a menu-based system, you may find yourself curiously poking around different Gopher servers just to see what's available. By all means, explore! While Telnet and FTP require you to know what you are looking for before you start, Gopher allows you to discover.

Another fascinating way to explore Gopherspace is to find a menu that reads Other Gopher and Information Servers and select it. (Almost every Gopher server offers this as a menu item somewhere.) Once it is selected you will see an option called All the Gopher Servers in the World. This is an alphabetical listing of every Gopher server that exists in the world. Whether you choose to browse by continent or name, start exploring around the globe. Remember, you cannot break the system, so go anywhere—you might be surprised by what you find.

Unlike other Internet services, Gopher doesn't actually keep the connection between computers open the whole time. When you Telnet or FTP to another machine, the two computers create a "virtual connection." That is, the computers establish a pipeline between them, which they use to pump data back and forth. The pipeline remains open until you log out or quit the session. Gopher, however, opens up the pipeline only long enough to grab a requested Gopher menu and display it for the user. It then closes the connection until the user makes another request. Occasionally when you select a Gopher menu item you will receive an error message saying Cannot connect to remote gopher server. This may happen even if you successfully connected ten seconds earlier. Realize that Gopher must reestablish the connection every time you make a menu selection. Thus, if you do see this type of error, clear it out (usually by hitting Return) and try again. Second attempts are often successful.

Veronica

There are ways that you can find information without having to navigate through numerous hierarchical levels. Veronica, which stands for Very Easy Rodent-Oriented Netwide Index to Computerized Archives, is the Gopher counterpart to the FTP tool Archie. Veronica searches Gopher menu titles based on keywords. When the search is complete you will see a list of menus that contain your search word or phrase. By selecting one of the resulting choices, you will automatically be connected to the Gopher server that maintains that particular menu.

Unlike Archie, Veronica is not run from the command line but rather from inside the Gopher system. So you'll need to find the menu choice that says Search Titles in Gopherspace Using Veronica. If you have a UNIX system, you can open a Gopher connection directly to a server that contains the Veronica menu. One such location is **gopher.micro.umn.edu**. Once connected, you can find Veronica within the Other Gopher and Information Servers menu. A sample Veronica screen is shown on the following page.

Did you notice that some menu items are listed more than once? This is because Veronica searches can be performed on several different net-

```
                Internet Gopher Information Client 2.0 p110

                Search titles in Gopherspace using veronica

      1.
      2.
      3.  About Veronica: Documents, Software, Index-Control Protocol/
      4.  Experimental Veronica Query Interface: Chooses Server for You!/
      5.  Find ONLY DIRECTORIES by Title word(s) (via NYSERNet) <?>
  --> 6.  Find ONLY DIRECTORIES by Title word(s) (via PSINet) <?>
      7.  Find ONLY DIRECTORIES by Title word(s) (via SCS Nevada ) <?>
      8.  Find ONLY DIRECTORIES by Title word(s) (via SUNET) <?>
      9.  Find ONLY DIRECTORIES by Title word(s) (via U. of Manitoba) <?>
     10.  Find ONLY DIRECTORIES by Title word(s) (via UNINETT..of Bergen) <?>
     11.  Find ONLY DIRECTORIES by Title word(s) (via University of Koeln)<?>
     12.  Find ONLY DIRECTORIES by Title word(s) (via University of Pisa) <?>
     13.  Frequently-Asked Questions (FAQ) about Veronica—July 29, 1994.
     14.  How to Compose Veronica Queries—June 23, 1994.
     15.  Search GopherSpace by Title word(s) (via NYSERNet) <?>
     16.  Search GopherSpace by Title word(s) (via PSINet) <?>
     17.  Search GopherSpace by Title word(s) (via SCS Nevada ) <?>
     18.  Search GopherSpace by Title word(s) (via SUNET) <?>

Press ? for Help, q to Quit, u to go up a menu              Page: 1/2
```

works. Do your best to pick the site geographically closest to you (this will help speed up the process). Once you make your selection, follow the prompts to enter your search word(s) and hit Return. In a few seconds you should have a list of menus that fit your description.

Be aware that the Veronica service is not yet local to all Gopher sites. Furthermore, some experimental Veronica systems are currently being tested. If you experience problems when trying to perform a Veronica query, simply try again at a later time.

Why Use Anything Else?

After looking at Gopher, you may wonder why you would ever want to use any of the older Internet services. The most compelling reason is that you cannot access everything on the Internet with Gopher. Some locations housing hundreds of files available by FTP or databases accessible through Telnet do not have Gopher servers. Other sites have only a fraction of their resources available through Gopher.

Gopher lends itself to documents that can be read online. Universities often use Gopher servers to post their college catalogs, academic calendars, school newspapers, and other relevant information. Numerous magazines and newspapers, such as *USA Today* and *The Chronicle of Higher Education*, have created Gopher servers that contain articles for browsing. But when it comes to finding shareware software or viewing digitized photographs, Gopher doesn't do the trick.

Another advantage of the older services is speed. If you know exactly what document you are looking for and where it is located, you may find it more useful to FTP a copy of it rather than view it with Gopher. Using FTP you can store a copy on your computer for later viewing rather than having to log in and run Gopher again.

Gopher's biggest weakness is its lack of organization. While there are many ways of accessing a Gopher server, information has not been organized in a logical structure. Gopher is like a flea market—there are plenty of treasures available to the diligent explorer, but there is no catalog to consult for guidance.

In the past year, Gopher has been almost completely superseded by the World Wide Web. Because the Web can do everything that Gopher could, plus much more, it has become the online publishing tool of choice. While some organizations still maintain Gopher sites, expect to see them phased out in the coming months.

Where to Begin

For an introductory Gopher server, the Virtual Reference Desk is an excellent choice. This server contains a wealth of reference information including a dictionary, a thesaurus, government documents, education resources, and even an electronic newsstand of online magazines. You can find the Virtual Reference Desk by typing **gopher** followed by its Internet address, which is **peg.cwis.uci.edu**. Alternately you can access this server under the USA hierarchy, in the California menu, by choosing the University of California, Irvine.

Gopher servers are also rife with Christian writings, ranging from the early church to contemporary authors. The Internet Wiretap contains numerous electronic books and documents including Bible translations, writings of Augustine and Chesterton, and the Anglican Book of Common Prayer. You can reach the Internet Wiretap by finding the USA hierarchy, selecting California, then choosing the Internet Wiretap. Its Internet address is **wiretap.spies.com**.

Many exciting treasures can be found abroad. The Durham Center for Theological Research, located in the United Kingdom, maintains a Gopher server with online biblical texts, liturgical documents, and even research about computer use in theological study. First travel to the Europe hierarchy, then select United Kingdom, then Durham University Information Service, then, finally, locate the department of theology. The address for Durham is **delphi.dur.ac.uk**.

Have you ever heard a song on the radio and wondered who recorded it or what album it's from? Alive 93.5 WHJT, an adult contemporary Christian music station owned and operated by Mississippi College, has placed its entire musical database on Gopher so users can search it for particular artists, songs, or albums. This helpful catalog, whose Internet address is simply **gopher.mc.edu**, can be located by selecting the USA hierarchy, choosing Mississippi, and then selecting Mississippi College.

Additional Gopher servers are listed in appendix C.

13

The World Wide Web

Are you familiar with the term *killer application?* A killer application, or killer app for short, is one that causes people to become interested in computer technology solely because of the influence of that one particular software product. Many people consider the electronic spreadsheet the first killer application for personal computers. Countless people purchased PCs solely to run Lotus 1-2-3. Recently, two products, actually an Internet service and complementary software product, were developed that many people consider to be the killer apps for the Internet. They possess more power than any of the Internet services that we have examined in the previous chapters, and they are even easier to use than Gopher. The Internet service is known as the World Wide Web, and the software product is called Netscape.

The World Wide What?

The World Wide Web is a second-generation Internet service that was developed a few years ago at the European Laboratory for Particle Physics. The Web is more than just an Internet tool; it is an attempt to harness the Internet's vast array of resources through a single hypertext, actually hypermedia, interface. The foundations of this interface are the Hypertext Markup Language, or HTML, and the Hypertext Transfer Protocol, or HTTP. Through the use of a program called a Web browser, users can navigate through the WWW (also called W3) without the burden of cumbersome Internet addresses or cryptic commands.

Developers wanted the vast and disparate information on the Internet to be made accessible to people in a way that frees them from the intimidating methods of UNIX. The resulting philosophy centers around a belief that people should be able to access information in a nonlinear fashion, mimicking the operation of the human brain. The Internet interface was created to reflect the way we often think and even research—namely, by word association. Finally, it was thought that the service should handle not only text, but also graphics, sound, file transfer, Gopher servers, and Telnet locations. In short, the Web was designed to be an all-purpose Internet interface that is both friendly and convenient to use. This was accomplished by building the Web around the concept of hypertext links.

What Is Hypertext?

To understand the concept of hypertext, think about how you read your Bible. Have you ever found yourself reading a passage in the Gospels where Jesus quotes from an Old Testament passage? Have you ever then looked up the original passage that Jesus is quoting? Perhaps you saw something else in that Old Testament chapter prompting you to flip to yet a different book. What have you done? You've jumped from one book to another based on a common subject.

Now let's say that you took that Bible and put it on a computer. As you read that Gospel passage, you notice that Jesus' quote from the Old Testament is highlighted. When you select that highlighted passage, the Bible automatically flips open to the Old Testament book so you can read the original quote in context. Such a Bible would be an example of hypertext—text linked together so that you can examine it in a nonlinear fashion. The highlighted passage would have a link, or pointer, to the Old Testament passage from which it was quoted. In fact, numerous passages would be linked to other passages for your exploration. Such a product could greatly simplify the cross-referencing aspect of Bible study.

The beauty of the WWW is that it does for the Internet what the aforementioned Bible example does for Scripture study. It allows you to leap from topic to topic and location to location without getting tangled in the navigational logistics. Thus you can spend your time using information rather than finding it.

WWW Home Pages

Sites wishing to participate in the Web develop a series of publicly accessible documents called home pages. Similar to Gopher servers, home pages

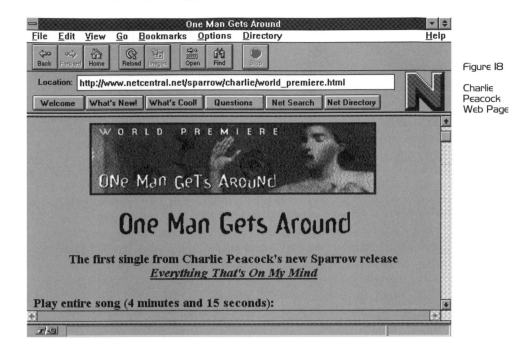

Figure 18

Charlie
Peacock
Web Page

include a plethora of information. Since home pages contain hypertext links, they can be joined to other home pages, documents, Gopher servers, or Internet resources. Home pages are often flashy, laced with fancy text, graphics, sound, and even video clips. Figure 18 shows a home page affiliated with CCM artist Charlie Peacock.

Because of the power of the Web, and also because home pages can be developed with little effort, the number of WWW home pages grew from a small handful to thousands within a matter of months. As you explore the Web you will quickly realize that you can spend hours crisscrossing the globe without ever typing in a single command. Expect to find some home pages that are refined and others clearly in developmental stages. Given the relative newness of the Web, you won't find everything completely polished and bug-free.

Uniform Resource Locators

The various Internet services are identified on the Web using Uniform Resource Locators. URLs provide a standard addressing scheme for locating anything on the Internet. Although the point and click interface of most

Web browsers allows you to avoid URLs altogether, they can often be a time-saver.

If you know the URL of a resource, you can instruct your Web browser to go directly to that particular home page rather than following a series of links to get there. Recalling our Bible example, you can open directly to any verse in the Bible if you know the verse reference. Wading through a series of cross-references is not always necessary. While hypertext links and biblical cross-referencing are both extremely useful, sometimes a direct route is preferred.

WWW home pages are named with the opening identifier **http://** followed by the address of the home page, usually in the form **www.organization.type**. For example, the Web home page of Loyola College in Maryland has the URL:

http://www.loyola.edu

Directory or file information can also be included in the URL.

http://unicks.calvin.edu/daily-bread/

This URL actually points to a directory called **daily-bread** found on Calvin College's computer system. It is a Web page containing the *Our Daily Bread* devotional.

What makes the URL such a powerful addressing tool is that it can also refer to other Internet services such as Gopher or Telnet. As you might guess, Gopher servers have the preface **gopher://** while Telnet sites are prefaced by **telnet://**. The following table provides examples of the various URL types.

Internet Service	Preface	URL Example	Description
World Wide Web	http://	http:// www.bethany.org/	Bethany Christian Services Web Page
Gopher	gopher://	gopher:// gopher.calvin.edu	Calvin College Gopher Server
FTP	ftp://	ftp:// ftp.ncsa.uiuc.edu	FTP Site that maintains the NCSA Mosaic software
Telnet	telnet://	telnet:// iclnet93.iclnet.org	Institute for Christian Leadership Bulletin Board

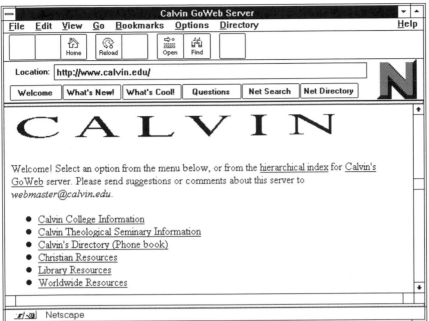

Figure 19

Netscape
Navigator,
Calvin
College

Web Browsers

Netscape

In order to access the Web you need to use a software package called a Web browser. The most popular is Netscape Navigator, a variation of Mosaic, the original graphical browser originally developed by the National Center for Supercomputing Applications (NCSA). Because of the popularity of Mosaic, NCSA licensed the technology to other companies to create commercial versions of the software. This has resulted in commercial products such as the Netscape Navigator and Spry AirMosaic. In addition, many commercial online services and proprietary Internet interface services have built customized, Netscape-like browsers for their systems. With so many flavors, the word *Netscape* has become a generic term for Web browser much in the way that Kleenex is commonly used to refer to facial tissue. Therefore, anything said about Netscape in this chapter applies equally to other graphical Web browsers.

Netscape is truly a revolution in the online world. Ten minutes worth of playing with Netscape will probably do more to convince you of the

Web's power and simplicity than ten thousand words written about it. Let's look at a picture of Netscape, shown in figure 19, to see how a Web page looks.

A couple of things should jump out at you. First, this doesn't look like the typical text-based UNIX interfaces that we saw in some of the previous chapters; the Web is much more approachable. Notice how the graphics and text are interspersed—it actually looks more like a book or magazine page than a computer screen. In fact, many people believe that the WWW is not only the future of the Internet, but also the future of publishing.

Did you notice that some of the words are underlined? On a color screen, the underlined words are further distinguished in a unique color, often blue. These are the hypertext links. When you click on a hypertext link, the Web browser will automatically jump to a related home page.

As mentioned previously, you can do all of your navigation in Netscape by pointing and clicking with your mouse. On the main screen you will notice that there are icons depicting a left arrow, a right arrow, and a house. The left arrow icon allows you to return to the previously viewed page. Actually, you can backtrack through numerous pages to retrace your steps or set forth in new directions. Correspondingly, the right arrow moves forward through the list of already visited sites. The home button will automatically load your default home page. When you first use Netscape, its default home page will probably be a Netscape demo document. You can change your default home page from the Netscape menu by modifying the appropriate configuration file. Check the online documentation for the specific procedure used by your software.

Other features on home pages include graphics and sound. Sound clips can be identified by a speaker icon. When you click on the speaker icon, a sound file will be downloaded onto your computer. If your system is equipped to play music and digitized sound, the sound file can then be run. Since digitized sound files are very large, a few seconds of sound will take a while to transmit. Often the size of a sound file is listed next to a speaker icon so you can determine if you'll have enough patience to retrieve it.

Using Netscape with a dial-up connection can be a painfully slow endeavor if you have a low modem speed. The biggest reason for this is because the graphics, called inline images, are large files that take a while to transmit. By turning off the inline images, you will significantly decrease the time required to load a home page. After turning off the inline images you can either click on an empty image box to have Netscape load a particular image, or turn on the inline images and reload the home page to view all of the graphics.

If you have favorite pages that you like to visit, you can create a hotlist and simply choose sites from it. As you visit new pages you can choose the "Add to hotlist" option and Netscape will automatically include the URL and description in your hotlist. Since a Netscape hotlist is merely a text file, you can also add URLs manually by editing that file.

If you connect to the Internet through a commercial online service or proprietary Internet interface service, you may already have Netscape, or an alternate graphical browser, available to you. Check with your provider about this. If, however, you connect using a SLIP/PPP account, then you can freely download Netscape from an anonymous FTP site and run it on top of your TCP/IP stack. The following chart shows where to acquire the software. Because file versions are updated regularly, check the online directory (using **dir** or **ls**) for the file name.

Platform	Developer	FTP Site	Directory
Windows	NCSA	`ftp.ncsa.uiuc.edu`	`/pub/PC/Mosaic`
Windows	Netscape	`ftp.netscape.com`	`/pub/netscape/windows`
Macintosh	NCSA	`ftp.ncsa.uiuc.edu`	`/pub/Mac/Mosaic`
Macintosh	Netscape	`ftp.netscape.com`	`/pub/netscape/mac`

Newer versions of operating systems will probably bundle Netscape (or another graphical Web browser) within their base software. As users upgrade to these operating systems, obtaining a Web browser will no longer be an issue.

Lynx

If you are unable to use a graphical Web browser because you connect to the Internet using a UNIX shell, you are not without hope. Lynx is a text-based browser that gives you full access to the text and hypertext links found on the WWW. The table below shows a Lynx version of the same Calvin College home page.

```
                                          Calvin GoWeb Server

   Calvin College


   Welcome! Select an option from the menu below, or from the
   hierarchical index for Calvin's GoWeb server. Please send
```

```
        suggestions or comments about this server to webmaster@calvin.edu.

          * Calvin College Information
          * Calvin Theological Seminary Information
          * Calvin's Directory (Phone book)
          * Christian Resources
          * Library Resources
          * Worldwide Resources


        Some of the resources found here are tools developed at Calvin.

        [IMAGE]

Commands: Use arrow keys to move, '?' for help, 'q' to quit, '<-' to go back
  Arrow keys: Up and Down to move. Right to follow a link; Left to go back.
  H)elp O)ptions P)rint G)o M)ain screen Q)uit /=search [delete]=history list
```

As you might guess, Lynx cannot support graphics, sound, or video clips. So although the home page information is identical, Lynx is less visually appealing than Netscape. Nevertheless, text-only access to the Web is better than no access at all. Most UNIX shell accounts make Lynx available; just type **lynx** at the command prompt to run the browser.

You can move around a home page in Lynx by using the up and down arrow keys or the tab key. The right and left arrow keys will follow the hypertext links downstream and upstream. Pressing **g** will give you the option to type in a specific URL that you'd like to visit. You also have the option of setting up a bookmark list, similar to Netscape's hotlist. Use the **v** command to view your bookmarks and the **a** command to add a site to the list. Lynx also has a thorough help system that can be accessed by typing **h**.

If you are limited to text but do not have Lynx on your system, a publicly accessible version of Lynx is available via Telnet.

Public Web Clients via Telnet
ukanaix.cc.ukans.edu
www.law.cornell.edu
www.njit.edu

Set your terminal type to VT100 emulation, Telnet to one of the addresses above, and enter **www** at the login prompt; you will log in and then be able to browse the Web (albeit slowly). Clearly, this is the least preferable option available, but it is better than nothing.

Good Places to Start

The beauty of the Web is that there is no one entry point. Your Web browser will probably load a home page for you automatically, giving you a convenient place to begin. Remember that most home pages have addresses that look like **www.organization.type**. This is the canonical form of a home page, so feel free to hunt for home pages by prefacing a known Internet address with **www**. For example, Bucknell University's Internet address is **bucknell.edu**. It is no surprise that their main home page has the address **www.bucknell.edu**.

The following list describes some excellent home page resources that you may wish to visit. Consult the Christian Internet Directory (appendix C) for further sites.

- *Christian Cyberspace Companion*—A site designed to complement this book, including a current online version of the subject-oriented Christian Internet Directory (appendix C). Visit this site to find pointers to Christian materials, offer feedback for future editions of *CCC*, or correspond with the author.
  http://www.bakerbooks.com/ccc/

- *Biblical Contradictions*—A Web page containing over 140 apparent biblical contradictions with responses to each.
  http://www.ugcs.caltech.edu/cgi-bin/webnews/read/ contradictions/0 (that's a zero)

- *Brother Mark's Christian Material*—Eclectic collection of Christian material ranging from theological discourses to cartoons.
  http://www.tit.fi/~mark/xian_1.html

- *Goshen*—Global Online Service Helping to Evangelize Nations. A large electronic gathering of Christian churches, ministries, organizations, companies, and programs.
  http://www.goshen.net

- *Netscape's What's Cool Page*—A page sponsored by the Netscape Corporation that lists cool Web sites worth visiting.
  http://www.netscape.com/home/whats-cool.html

- *Scrolls from the Dead Sea*—An electronic museum exhibit featuring digitized pictures of the scrolls, articles about their translation, and historical information about the Qumran community.

  `http://sunsite.unc.edu/expo/deadsea.scrolls.exhibit/in-tro.html`

- *The Very Official Charlie Peacock Internet Site*—A Web site that, unlike most celebrity pages, is actually run by Charlie Peacock himself. The page includes sound clips, song lyrics, and personal comments.

  `http://www.netcentral.net/sparrow/charlie/index.html`

- *World Wide Web Bible Gateway*—An extensive online project offering multiple translations of Scripture, in many different languages, searchable by keyword. Even includes footnotes and cross-references!

  `http://www.gospelcom.net/bible`

- *Yahoo Subject Guide*—A Web library with pointers to over 30,000 home pages organized by subject.

  `http://www.yahoo.com`

14

Looking Ahead

Summarizing the world of cyberspace is nearly impossible. The cyberspace frontier is changing on a daily basis as increasing numbers of users come online. The technology is continually advancing, and the opportunities seem limitless. But where is it all going? When will we arrive, and what will the online world look like once we get there? And for that matter, will we ever arrive? Although there are no clear answers to these questions, there are some issues worth mentioning.

The Future of Cyberspace

Despite the recent flurry of activity surrounding the Internet and the cyberspace community, we are really only at the beginning of this journey. While the mere thought of reading the Library of Congress card catalog, visiting an electronic museum exhibit of the Dead Sea Scrolls, or communicating with friends overseas without leaving your house would have seemed impossible only a few years ago, they are only the beginning of online technology.

Imagine a missionary being able to send and receive e-mail from a notepad-sized computer in a village *without* phones. How about being able to witness, live, your grandson taking his first steps, even though he lives in Los Angeles and you are in Boston? Maybe you will send the members of your church a video clip of your newborn daughter, announcing the details of her birth. Perhaps you would like to take a tour of Jerusalem, complete with video, sound, and even a tour guide, without ever leaving your living room. You might even engage in a lively theological debate with classmates scattered throughout the world, being able to see and hear them, while you work on your master's degree in theology from your den.

All of these scenarios are possible and even feasible in the near future. A number of obstacles, however, must be overcome before technology can advance in these directions.

Obstacles and Questions

Just as railroads, highway systems, and airplanes opened up the opportunity for mass transit, there must also be a means of transporting mass information. While the Internet is suited for e-mail, discussion groups, and the occasional photo or sound clip, it is not equipped to handle hundreds of millions of people corresponding by live video. It would be similar to draining an ocean with a garden hose. There is simply too much data to fit through a very small pipe.

The National Information Infrastructure, or information superhighway, is an initiative intended to spur the development of a backbone capable of handling the ever-increasing demand for information. Such an infrastructure would resemble the interstate highway system or telephone system as it would link geographical sites. Given the expressed desire of numerous companies toward such an infrastructure, it is not a question of whether such a backbone will be built; it is simply a matter of when and how.

Once the backbone is developed, there is still the issue of the home. What good does it do you if there is an eight-lane highway close to your house, but no connecting roads to get to it? As the demands for information transport increase, the wiring system that connects to your house will need to increase as well. Both telephone and cable television companies are working feverishly to address this need. Whether fiber optic cable, phone lines, or cable television connections become the medium of choice, this issue must be solved before everyone can travel the information superhighway.

Another hurdle to be cleared is the difficulty of use. With graphical interfaces on many commercial systems and Internet tools such as Mosaic, cyberspace navigation is becoming easier. But even today you still need to be able to work with a computer and often even wade through cryptic UNIX commands in order to get around the Internet. The interface must be simplified and made more intuitive. Until the online world becomes as easy to understand as a telephone or television, its potential will be limited.

There is still much debate regarding the preferred vehicle for future navigation in cyberspace. One view says computers will continue to be the vehicle of choice, while another view insists that television sets will become the means. The latter group envisions home banking, movies on demand, and video mail correspondence occurring through the television set. Rather than standard computer keyboards, we will use customized remote controls.

Besides offering cyberspace access, someone must ensure that there is worthwhile information to access. What types of information should be available through such an information superhighway? Who will create and maintain it? Will there be information providers such as CompuServe and CBS, or will everybody be able to make information available? This leads to questions of control. What will prevent someone from using the new technology to mass-distribute child pornography? How about issues of privacy? Who, if anyone, will govern such an information system?

Social and cultural issues are also factors. How do we work and play in an increasingly global marketplace? What role will the new information frontier play in international negotiations, trade, education, and even missionary work? By allowing people access to such a vast amount of information at home, will we become a de-socialized community? Will an information superhighway produce a country of high-tech, well-informed couch potatoes?

Finally, there is the question of money. Who will pay for all of this progress? What, if anything, will be done to ensure that everyone will have access to the technology? How will the responsibilities be divided between the government and the private sector?

Christians and Cyberspace

Regardless of how all of these issues are resolved, the unfolding of the Information Age offers great challenges and opportunities for Christians. We are called to glorify God and work for the advancement of his kingdom—this call extends to cyberspace. As we have seen, some Christians have already seized the opportunities of this new frontier. Cyberspace has enabled believers to cross social, geographical, and denominational boundaries and has done a great deal to bring together the body of Christ.

The Information Age also poses many challenges to Christians. Computer bulletin boards and the Internet have been used to increase the exchange of pornography, both legal and illegal, across the country. Because of the infancy of much of this technology, young people are often more familiar with cyberspace than their parents. Subsequently, many unsuspecting children have been exposed to pornography or verbally assaulted while online. Just as believers are attempting to use online resources to further Christ's kingdom, others clearly have less godly intentions. Make no mistake about it, the Evil One is keenly interested in using cyberspace for his ends.

Because the online world is still changing rapidly, now is the time for the church to determine how it wants to use these opportunities. If Christians retreat from our call to be salt and light, then the foreseeable future of cyberspace could be much like that of television. Praise God for endeavors like Goshen, Christian BBSs, Christianity Online, and the Christian Interactive Network for seeing the potential of the online world and stepping out boldly to shape this new environment.

We know that cyberspace will continue to affect our lives, but we don't know precisely how. Online connections will likely become as commonplace as cars, telephones, and televisions. Now is the time to start participating. Not only is there much to be gained, but there is also plenty of opportunity to give.

See you online!

Appendix A

Parental Guidance Suggested

In the beginning, God declared that all of his creation was good. Soon after, however, sin defaced that goodness. The results of the fall are seen in all aspects of society, including the online world. Despite the numerous benefits of cyberspace, it is far from perfect. Christians should be prepared for the sin-scarred reality they will face online.

Pornography

Pornography, both legal and illegal, is extremely prevalent on the Internet. Computer bulletin board systems and commercial online services are no exception. Tracking surveys report that sexually explicit USENET groups, from the titillating to the perverse, are consistently among the most popular groups visited. These groups contain explicit stories, X-rated movie reviews, escort services, and other sordid topics. Digitized pornographic pictures are also popular online resources. Some BBSs specialize in legal adult material, while others are used for the distribution of child pornography. Even CompuServe, a mainstream commercial service, has a *Playboy* section complete with "meet the playmate" discussions and magazine photos.

Unlike in video stores, cyberspace travelers aren't required to show proof of age before acquiring pornographic material. This makes it difficult to prevent children from gaining exposure to such material. Many services, even the ones that normally prohibit explicit material, consider the Internet to be external to their system and thus do not block access to explicit information. However, you need not fear accidentally stumbling across pornography. Generally, it has been corralled into cyberspace back rooms that must be intentionally entered to acquire pornographic material.

Just as adult videos helped to fuel the video revolution, many believe that pornography will be a major force in the expansion of the online world.

Child Solicitation

The presence of pornography is generally a passive issue; those who want the material must search to acquire it. Unfortunately, there is an active side to the information superhighway red-light district. Some adults, knowing that parents are often not online, will solicit children. They may ask for nude photographs from, tell explicit stories to, or request a personal meeting with an unwitting youngster. They may even pose as children themselves attempting to lure minors into personal encounters. Such incidents are most likely to occur on commercial online services with their instant messages and chat functions.

Practical Suggestions

While there is no way to shelter children from all evil, parents can take some simple steps to protect their children.

- *Spend time online without your children.* By checking out online services before allowing your children access, you will be more aware of the various hazards.
- *Block objectionable material if possible.* Some services, including America Online and Prodigy, allow parents to restrict which features children may access.
- *Talk to your children about the online dangers.* Make them aware of cyberspace hazards and clearly set their boundaries.
- *Get to know what services your children use.* Spend time with them exploring various online services and applications. Find out their favorite online areas. Encourage them toward uplifting and educational material.
- *Do not give out personal information on a public service.* By posting your address, phone number, or the name of the child's school, you make it easier for predators to target your children.

- *Never allow children to arrange phone calls or face-to-face meetings with those they encounter online.* Given the faceless nature of cyberspace, you don't really know anything about the other person.
- *Never reply to offensive or suggestive e-mail messages.* Instead, forward them on to the System Administrator for official action.
- *Monitor, and limit, the amount of time children spend online.* Despite the numerous benefits of cyberspace, online adventures are no substitute for real ones.

Pornography on the Web

As discussed in chapter 13, the World Wide Web has revolutionized the Internet. Many organizations, from small churches to international corporations, have discovered that by publishing on the Web, they can easily reach millions of people. Unfortunately, the pornographers have also been quick to capitalize on the Web's power. Furthermore, the presence of mainstream companies online, such as Playboy and Penthouse, has dramatically altered the electronic landscape. While online individuals have been making pornography available for years, they lack the financial motivation (and resources) of large companies.

The rapid developments in online pornography have caused division within the pro-family community. Some believe that new legislations must be passed to punish those who distribute pornography, while others are concerned that strict controls could ultimately backfire and hurt legitimate online communication. Clearly Christians need to engage in the current debate to ensure that Biblical morality is upheld. In the interim, a number of software packages have been developed which allow parents to prevent children from accessing questionable material on the Web. Two of the leading products are SurfWatch and CyberPatrol. For additional information, contact Surfwatch at (800) 458-6600 or Microsystems Software (creator of CyberPatrol) at (800) 626-8515.

In Perspective

Like the real world, the online world is full of hazards. To avoid cyberspace because of such problems would be like avoiding books because some bookstores carry explicit material. It is precisely for this reason that Christians should be in cyberspace, to serve as salt and light in a fallen online society. By becoming active in cyberspace while it is still in its developmental stages, we can influence how such concerns will be resolved.

Appendix B

Christian BBS List

This list provides phone numbers of Christian bulletin board systems in most area codes throughout the country. It is intended as a representative sample to get you started. Given the volatility of BBSs, some numbers may be defunct.

201—Northeast New Jersey
Stained Glass201-762-2846

202—Washington, D.C.
Alpha & Omega202-767-0406

203—Connecticut
Father John's203-934-4641

205—Alabama
Christian Apologetics Network
   205-808-0763
The Family Smorgasboard205-744-0943
Southern Cross205-492-7685

206—Western Washington
Armor of God206-440-7499
Christian Research206-244-6797
Kingdom Come206-823-1267
The Rock206-698-7308

207—Maine
Opus Dei207-780-6567

208—Idaho
The Upper Room208-343-5817

210—Southern Texas
Calvary210-658-4519
Catholic Access Network210-423-1574

213—Los Angeles, California
Christ's Corner213-938-6579
Heaven's Door213-936-0365

214—Northeast Texas
New Creations214-203-1514
Wisdom Research214-539-9878

215—Southeast Pennsylvania
Empty Tomb215-677-4457
Roman Catholic215-365-0825

216—Northeast Ohio
God's Work216-322-6047
Voice in the Wilderness II216-741-6244

217—South Central Illinois
God & Country217-877-8728
The Lighthouse217-735-2251

219—Northern Indiana
Christian Connection219-464-9164

Restoration Rock219-926-2060
Spreading the Word219-232-0248

301—Southern and Western Maryland
John 3:16301-208-0855
Alpha & Omega301-735-6789
Maryland Catholic301-596-3230
PhileoNet301-870-0399

302—Delaware
Missions Possible302-678-9005

303—Northern and Western Colorado
Christian Connection303-352-5013
Pure Word303-669-5935
Sound Doctrine303-680-7209

304—West Virginia
International Christian Computer
    304-258-5156
Sword of the Spirit304-736-4715

305—Southeast Florida
Christian Computer Users Group
    305-726-5434
Genesis Network II305-698-9228
House of Ichthus305-360-2991

308—Western Nebraska
Church Chatters308-872-6112

309—West Central Illinois
The Pastor's Board309-693-9475

310—Los Angeles, California
Christ Connection310-398-7804
Equipping the Saints310-630-7090
Servant Christian310-371-0251

312—Chicago, Illinois
Jesus People USA312-878-6040

313—Eastern Michigan
A Call For Papers313-535-0842
Catholic Mail Box313-631-6870
Jesus Is Lord313-537-9452
One Way Christian313-537-1161

314—Eastern Missouri
Family Connection314-544-4628
Messianic Jewish Net314-227-6885
St. Louis Christian314-947-0895

316—Southern Kansas
Central Truth Ministries316-542-5263
The Fawnetta316-721-1005

317—Central Indiana
Agape Family Net317-664-3312
Apostolic Info Service317-781-7712
Logos317-473-7562

318—Western Louisiana
Bible Bulletin Board318-949-1456
Christian Evangel Network318-397-2987

401—Rhode Island
Sword of the Spirit401-433-2036

402—Eastern Nebraska
Light House402-597-2451

404—Northern Georgia
The GraceNet404-979-8240

**405—Southern and Western
    Oklahoma**
Highway to Heaven405-366-1007
Light of the City405-321-1333
Trinity405-692-2289

406—Montana
Butte Christian406-494-8012

407—Eastern Florida
Bloomunit for Homeschoolers
    407-687-8712
Christian Computers407-240-1460
Genesis407-582-1972

408—Central Coastal California
Logos408-899-4552
Silicon Valley Christian Connection
    408-246-7002
Theology Net408-229-0706

409—Southeast Texas
Agape Way409-753-2014
GreenTree409-736-2321
The Word409-982-2218

410—Eastern Maryland
Biblical Resource Network410-515-4860
Harvester410-828-4572
Maryland Catholic410-997-5262

412—Western Pennsylvania
Ecclesia Place412-741-5519
LifeLine412-829-7955
Methodist412-683-1377

414—Eastern Wisconsin
Christian Connection414-541-6105

415—West Bay Area California
Catholic Info Net415-387-3251
Salt and Light415-368-0790

417—Southwest Missouri
Alpha-Omega417-862-5584

501—Arkansas
For God & Country501-843-2614
Genesis501-267-9600
Holy Loch501-246-7002
Warriors for Christ501-931-1177

502—Western Kentucky
Ecunet502-569-8501

503—Oregon
A Voice in the Wilderness503-239-5958
Institute for Christian Leadership
   503-598-7884

504—Eastern Louisiana
Christian Backbone & CDN HQ's
   504-878-3027
The Christian Connection504-667-4735

505—New Mexico
Keys to the Kingdom505-762-8879

508—Eastern Massachusetts
The Lighthouse508-892-8857
Serenity Board508-740-0351
The Way of Life508-537-4118

509—Eastern Washington
Christian Education509-325-8639

510—East Bay Area California
Alpha & Omega510-278-0297
Church510-754-4520
Ecclesia Online510-526-6584

512—Southern Texas
Inspiration512-452-6350
Kevin Remote Access512-928-2279
Maranatha512-326-1757
RoBBS512-443-5609

513—Southwest Ohio
Mission Communication513-434-8355
Peace Net513-751-4009

515—Central Iowa
The Bible Board515-243-8939
Good News505-961-5693

601—Mississippi
Chi Rho601-896-6086
Newlife601-627-5582

602—Arizona
Cornerstone602-899-9329
El-Shaddai602-839-3966
Pros Apologian602-963-3739
Standing Word602-981-2099

603—New Hampshire
Nor'Easter603-432-6711

606—Eastern Kentucky
Bible Study II606-744-6079

608—Southwest Wisconsin
Lighthouse Christian608-837-6420

609—Southern New Jersey
Alpha Omega609-692-9366

Freedom Infonet609-586-4847

610—Southeast Pennsylvania
The Rose of Sharon610-384-5138

612—Central Minnesota
GraceNet612-474-0724

614—Southeast Ohio
The Fisherman's Net614-837-0400
Project Thunder614-622-9027

615—Eastern Tennessee
Bible Bulletin Board615-579-5692
Charis Christian615-966-7653
Christian Connection615-352-2479
Credenda/Agenda615-283-4432
Day Star615-896-6870
Kerygma615-391-5771

616—Western Michigan
BibleStudy616-372-9946
Christian Home Education616-966-0861

618—Southern Illinois
Truth Net618-937-3962

619—Imperial Valley, California
Abba II619-487-7746
Catholic Information Network
   619-287-5828
Free Zone619-582-2402
The Shepherd's Flock619-630-0340

702—Nevada
The Lord's Way702-898-5966

703—Northern and Western Virginia
IXOYE703-381-9758
To His Glory703-573-8652
Trinity703-330-0078

704—Western North Carolina
Anglican Episcopal Network704-553-7673
The Christian Star704-598-9611
Gordon Conwell704-552-8160

706—Northern Georgia
The Potter's House706-637-9276

707—North Coastal California
Born Again707-763-8287
Corpus Christi707-935-6447
Covenant Keeper707-987-3022

708—Northeast Illinois
Chicago Area Computer Center
   708-739-0075
Christian Connection708-540-9383
Computers for Christ708-362-7875
Familynet Echogate708-230-9068
Gospel Outreach708-934-1649

712—Western Iowa
Exegete's Haven712-758-3483

713—Houston, Texas
Burk Ministries713-947-2795
The Christian Chat713-451-8406
The Corner Stone713-344-0815
The Pentecostal713-641-3058
Set Free713-324-4421

714—Orange County, California
The Battle Cry!714-521-5430
Christian Central714-971-1564
In His Service714-279-6987
Last Days714-526-3210
Saltshaker714-850-1539
Shofar714-838-3837

715—Northern Wisconsin
Promised Land715-387-1339

716—Western New York
Island in the Son716-865-8843

717—East Central Pennsylvania
Church Online717-393-9966

718—New York City, New York
FamilyNet718-295-1835
Fordham Jesuit718-817-5500

NewLife: The Promised Land
 718-562-1946

719—Southeast Colorado
The Retreat719-574-5119

803—South Carolina
The Glory Bound803-592-5208
The Lighthouse803-949-0199
SouBaptist803-370-2997

804—Southeast Virginia
Israel's Hope804-468-1375
Servant of the Lord804-590-2161

805—South Central California
HIS Board805-652-1478
The Lighthouse805-272-1812
Spring of Life805-296-7817

806—North Panhandle Texas
Agape806-795-9003

810—North Eastern Michigan
King of Creation810-356-0021
New Life810-795-5829

813—Southwest Florida
Jesus On-Line813-688-1470
One Way813-621-7547
Tetragrammaton813-327-2497

815—Northern Illinois
Revelations815-727-3398

816—Northwest Missouri
Christian Word816-587-5360
The Rock816-931-1257

817—North Central Texas
Alpha Zeta817-246-3058
Berean Bible Quest II817-526-5217
The Fortress817-763-5583

The Mission Board817-627-8037

901—Western Tennessee
Grace901-452-0168
NewLife Christian Network901-387-1768

903—Northeast Texas
Maranatha903-465-4022

904—Northern Florida
Guiding Light904-744-9991
Living Waters904-789-4152
The Rock904-738-7102

907—Alaska
Alcon907-522-3806

909—Southern California
In His Service909-279-6987
Solid Rock909-785-9176

910—Eastern North Carolina
Thief in the Night910-486-5427

913—Northern Kansas
Aslan's Den913-592-2937

915—Western Texas
Rio Christian915-566-4242

916—Northern California
The Field of Boaz Christian916-992-0440
The Genesis916-965-9361
Powerhouse916-343-2933

918—Northeast Oklahoma
Christian Depot918-832-1063
The Cross Connection918-747-4924
High Counsel918-357-1327

919—Eastern North Carolina
White Harvest Software919-846-2141

Appendix C

Christian Internet Directory

This appendix contains mailing lists, newsgroups, Gopher servers, and Web pages relevant to the Christian community. Where you see instructions for subscribing, put your given name in place of *Chris Christian*. Visit `http://www.bakerbooks.com/ccc/` on the World Wide Web for the latest updates to this appendix.

Abortion

talk.abortion
Secular discussion group to debate the abortion issue.

Adoption

Bethany Christian Services
`gopher.bethany.org`
What We Do—Nationwide—Adoption Services

Bethany Christian Services
`http://www.bethany.org/`
Introduction to Bethany Christian Services.

Anglican/Episcopal

The American University
`listserv.american.edu`
(USA—Washington D.C.—The American University)
Anglican Files

Anglican
`listserv@american.edu`

Send a one line message text (not subject line) that says:
`subscribe anglican Chris Christian`
Non-hostile environment for discussion about Anglican/Episcopal beliefs and practices. Non-Anglicans are welcome but attacks and debates about the Episcopal church are not.

Anglicans Online
`http://infomatch.com/~haibeck/anglican.html`
Unofficial site for the Anglican Church of Canada, complete with Synod notes, sermons, newsletters, church information, and other resources.

Episcopal
`majordomo@list.us.net`
Send a one line message text (not subject line) that says:
`subscribe episcopal Chris Christian`
Discussion group for Episcopalians, primarily focused on those in the Washington, D.C., area.

General Convention of the Episcopal Church
`http://xymox.palo-alto.ca.us/epi/`

Minutes from church convention.

Internet Wiretap
wiretap.spies.com
(USA—California—Internet Wiretap)
Wiretap Online Library—Religion—
Anglican

Methodist-Anglican Society
http://www.york.ac.uk/~socs161/
University of York Christian society to help
believers deepen their understanding of God
and apply their faith in their daily lives.

Religion in England
http://www.iris.brown.edu/iris/RIE/
Religion_OV.html
An overview of England's religious traditions
with particular emphasis on the Church of England and the Roman Catholic Church. Additional information about the Bible, Protestant
denominations, and non-Christian religions
are also online.

Apologetics

Apologia-L
majordomo@netcom.com
Send a one line message text (not subject line)
that says:
subscribe apologia-l
A discussion group of Christian apologetics
where the Bible is understood to be absolute
and the ultimate standard.

Biblical Contradictions
http://www.ugcs.caltech.edu/cgi-bin/
webnews/read/contradictions/0
A series of over 140 apparent biblical contradictions that originally appeared in the soc.reli-
gion.christian USENET group. Included is the
purported contradiction, a resolution to the
contradiction, and comments about the resolution. An index and feedback option is also
present.

Christian Apologetics
file://gate.net/pub/users/copeland/html/
ca/ca.html
Evidences for the Christian faith in a hypertext
format.

Christian Research Institute Journal Articles
file://iclnet93.iclnet.org/pub/resources/
text/cri/cri-jrnl/crijnl.html

Articles from the *CRI Journal* provided by the
Institute for Christian Leadership.

Pro-Christ
server@pro-christ.cts.com
Send a one line message text (not subject line)
that says:
help
An archive of files from the Balm in Gilead
Ministries accessible through e-mail. The help
request will give instructions on how to access
the files.

Questions and Answers about Religion and Christianity
http://cruciform.cid.com/werdna/cgi-bin/
webnews/read/q-and-a/0
A series of questions and answers about religion, and particularly Christianity, written and
collected by a Christian who has asked them
himself. In addition to his responses, there is
opportunity to answer them for yourself.

Unravelling Wittgenstein's Net
http://www.webcom.com:80/~ctt/
A Christian think tank that serves as a central
point of intellectual and scholarly discussion
about the Christian faith.

Art

The Art House
http://www.netcentral.net/
arthouse.index.html
Home page of the Art House, a non-profit organization dedicated to cultivating the Christian mind in the field of art.

Christian Arts
arts-req@dfcuk.demon.co.uk
Discussion list about Christian arts, primarily
drama, dance, and movement, sponsored by
Dance for Christ.

Dance for Christ
http://jesus.ox.ac.uk/~rmedcalf/dfc1.html
A Christian arts group based in England that
communicates the Christian faith using dance,
mime, and movement.

Baptist

Baptist
listserv@ukcc.uky.edu

Send a one line message text (not subject line) that says:

`subscribe baptist Chris Christian`

Discussion list for all aspects related to the Baptist experience. Topics include doctrine, practice, denominations, opinions, and inquiries.

Mississippi College

`gopher.mc.edu`

(USA—Mississippi—Mississippi College) Libraries and Reference Services—Christian Internet Resources—The Baptist Press

SBPress

`listserv@iclnet93.iclnet.org`

Send a one line message text (not subject line) that says:

`subscribe christian@church.org`

to the above address and put your Internet address in place of `christian@church.org`.

Press releases from the Southern Baptist Press.

Bible

Abilene Christian University

`bible.acu.edu`

(USA—Texas—College of Biblical and Family Studies, Abilene Christian University) Bible and Theological Information

Basic English Commentaries Project

`http://www.aiai.ed.ac.uk/~jkk/wycliffe-words.html`

Information about a Wycliffe project to make Bible commentaries available to third-world pastors in their own languages using volunteers with computers.

Bible-L

`listserv@gitvml.gatech.edu`

Send a one line message text (not subject line) that says:

`subscribe bible-l Chris Christian`

Open, unmoderated discussion about the Bible.

Biblical Contradictions

`http://www.ugcs.caltech.edu/~werdna/contradictions/contradictions.html`

A series of over 140 apparent biblical contradictions that originally appeared in the soc.religion.christian USENET group. Included is the purported contradiction, a resolution to the contradiction, and comments about the resolution. An index and feedback option is also present.

Internet Wiretap

`wiretap.spies.com`

(USA—California—Internet Wiretap) Wiretap Online Library—Articles—Biblical Timeline

Scrolls from the Dead Sea

`http://sunsite.unc.edu/expo/deadsea.scrolls.exhibit/intro.html`

An online exhibit of the Dead Sea scrolls based on the Library of Congress exhibit. The online version includes pictures of the scrolls, historical information about the Qumran community, and articles about the scrolls.

The World Wide Web Bible Gateway

`http://www.calvin.edu/cgi-bin/bible`

An online searchable Bible gateway that allows you to search multiple versions, such as the KJV and Darby, based on verse reference or keywords.

Bible Study

B-Greek

`majordomo@virginia.edu`

Send a one line message text (not subject line) that says:

`subscribe b-greek`

Focused on the scholarly study of the New Testament in Greek. While anyone can subscribe, participants should have at least a basic proficiency in Greek. Sponsored by the Center for Christian Study, an independent Christian ministry at the University of Virginia.

B-Hebrew

`majordomo@virginia.edu`

Send a one line message text (not subject line) that says:

`subscribe b-hebrew`

Focused on the scholarly study of the Old Testament in Hebrew. While anyone can subscribe, participants should have at least a basic proficiency in Hebrew and Aramaic. Sponsored by the Center for Christian Study, an independent Christian ministry at the University of Virginia.

Bible

`majordomo@virginia.edu`

Send a one line message text (not subject line) that says:

```
subscribe bible
```

Discussion group for those learning how to study the Bible. Participants should consider the Bible to be authoritative. Sponsored by the Center for Christian Study, an independent Christian ministry at the University of Virginia.

Bstudy-L

```
listserv@admin.humberc.on.ca
```

Send a one line message text (not subject line) that says:

```
subscribe bstudy-l Chris Christian
```

Moderated discussion about the Bible and its application in life. Discussion presumes that participants hold to the authority of Scripture.

Bible Study Resources

```
ad873@freenet.carleton.ca
```

Frequently asked questions about Bible study skills, tools, resources, and techniques.

Center for Biblical Literacy Online

```
http://www.cbl.org/cbl
```

A "virtual campus" created by the Center for Biblical Literacy's School of Theological Studies. CBL offers undergraduate and graduate programs in biblical studies through distance learning.

Executable Outlines Series

```
ftp://gate.net/pub/users/copeland/html/
exeout.html
```

Collection of Bible study guides and sermon outlines presented in a computer program.

Expository Files

```
ftp://gate.net/pub/users/copeland/ef/
00index.html
```

Monthly publication dedicated to biblical investigation.

Grace Notes Home Page

```
http://www.realtime.net/~wdoud/
```

A Christian publications ministry for distributing Bible study resources.

Johnlitr

```
listserv@univscvm.csd.scarolina.edu
```

Send a one line message text (not subject line) that says:

```
subscribe johnlitr Chris Christian
```

A discussion group for those interested in dialogue about the Gospel of John.

Koinonia House

```
http://www.khouse.org/khouse/index.html
```

Koinonia House is a publishing ministry oriented toward the development of materials to improve the study and application of Scripture.

Logos Research Systems

```
http://islander.whidbey.net/~logos/
```

Web page sponsored by Logos Research Systems, a developer of computerized Bible software.

Prophecy

```
prophecy@cyberearth.mscl.msstate.edu
```

Discussion of prophecy and the second coming.

soc.religion.christian.bible-study

Discussion of all aspects of the Bible. This includes not only the 66 books recognized in the King James Bible but also the apocryphal/deuterocanonical books included in the Roman Catholic Bible and books recognized by the Orthodox Churches. Topics are not limited to any theological or denominational perspective.

Soc.Religion.Christian.Bible-Study Mail Server

```
listproc@spss.com
```

Send a one line message text (not subject line) that says:

```
GET BIBLE filename
```

to the above address and put the name of the FAQ in place of filename.

Mail server to distribute a variety of FAQs and studies pertinent to soc.religion.christian.bible-study. The following files are available:

`Bible.List` Information on Bible versions and their origins.

`BibleStudy.Charter` Charter of soc.religion.christian.bible-study.

`E-Bible.FAQ` Information relating to electronic Bibles.

`Eschatology.1` A study in eschatology by Tom Albrecht.

`Genealogies` Discussion of genealogies in Matthew and Luke.

`Genesis.Accounts` Are the Genesis accounts in chronological order?

`Genesis.Days` How long were the days of creation?

`Genesis.Gap` Is there a gap between Genesis 1:1 and 1:2?

Genesis.Long_Days Defense of the day-age view.

Isaiah714 Commentary on the prophecy in Isaiah 7:14.

Judas.Death Harmonization of Matthew 27 and Acts 1 (the death of Judas).

Judas.Death.Crit Criticism of Judas.Death FAQ.

Moderator.View Moderator's viewpoint/ theology.

NT.Dating Information on authors and dates of writing of NT books.

NT.Canon Information on early canonical collections of NT books.

OnLine.Bibles List of online Bibles available.

Policy Moderator's policies for soc.religion.christian.bible-study.

Psalm.Numbering Psalm numbering guide.

Trinity A Study on the doctrine of the Trinity by Frank DeCenso.

Soc.Religion.Christian.Bible-Study WWW Server
http://www.spss.com/bible.html
Web page containing documents relevant to the soc.religion.christian.bible-study USENET news group. Includes Frequently Asked Questions, charter, and moderator information.

University of Pennsylvania
gopher.upenn.edu
(USA—Pennsylvania—University of Pennsylvania)
Gopher Servers at Penn —Center for Computer Analysis of Texts—Archives of the Center for Computer Analysis of Texts—Religion—Biblical

Unravelling Wittgenstein's Net
http://www.webcom.com:80/~ctt/
A Christian think tank that serves as a central point of intellectual and scholarly discussion about the Christian faith.

Vanderbilt Divinity Special Collections
vuinfo.vanderbilt.edu
(USA—Tennessee—Vanderbilt)
Library Resources and Services—About Libraries at Vanderbilt University—Divinity Library

Books

Baker Book House
http://www.bakerbooks.com
Web page developed by Baker Book House, a leading evangelical Christian publisher.

Calvin College
gopher.calvin.edu
(USA—Michigan—Calvin College)
Library Resources—Electronic Journals and Full-Text "Books"

Christian Classics Ethereal Books
http://www.cs.pitt.edu:80/~planting/books/
A collection of classical Christian books in electronic format. Titles include *Easton's Bible Dictionary*, *John Calvin on the Christian Life*, *Religious Affections* by Jonathan Edwards, and *Matthew Henry's Concise Commentary on the Whole Bible.*

Christian Cyberspace Companion
http://www.bakerbooks.com/ccc/
A site designed to complement this book, including a current online version of the subject-oriented Christian Internet Directory (appendix C). Visit this site to find pointers to Christian materials, offer feedback for future editions of *CCC*, or correspond with the author.

E-Text Archives
gopher.etext.org
Gutenberg.

Gutenberg E-Text Web Page
http://med-amsa.bu.edu/Gutenberg/Welcome.html
A project to make books freely available in an electronic format. The eclectic mix of titles ranges from *Peter Pan* to the *CIA World Factbook;* Christian titles include the King James Bible and works by G. K. Chesterton.

Internet Wiretap
wiretap.spies.com
(USA—California—Internet Wiretap)
Electronic Books at Wiretap

Online Books Page
http://www.cs.cmu.edu:8001/Web/books.html
Front page for an index of hundreds of online books, including Christian and secular titles.

Pointing the Way: A Guide to Christian Literature on the Internet

http://www.calvin.edu/pw.html

A Web page developed by the Not Just Bibles team in coordination with the Institute for Christian Leadership. The page is designed to provide a central directory to Christian Literature. Pointers include a variety of Bible translations, books, articles, and various creeds and confessions.

Springs of Life

http://emall.com/Springs/SOL1.html

An online Christian store that contains books, videos, clothing, and other products.

University of North Carolina Religious Texts

calypso.oit.unc.edu

(USA—North Carolina—UNC)
Worlds of SunSITE—Religious Texts

Brethren

Christian Brethren

majordomo@cs.dal.ca

Send a one line message text (not subject line) that says:

subscribe cb

Moderated discussion group by and about those who belong to the Christian Brethren.

Christian Peacemaker Teams Network

listserv@uci.com

Send a one line message text (not subject line) that says:

subscribe cptnet Chris Christian

Discussion among Christians working for justice and peace sponsored by the Mennonite church and Church of the Brethren.

Campus Ministry

Auburn Wesley Foundation

http://www.eng.auburn.edu/users/jasonc/wesleyhome.html

Page for the Wesley Foundation at Auburn University.

The Bridge Magazine

bridge@linus.cs.ohiou.edu

Christian publication by student groups at Ohio University.

The Bridge

http://linus.cs.ohiou.edu/~bridge

Coalition of Christian student groups at Ohio University. Web page includes information about the various campus groups and their self-titled magazine.

Campus CrossWalk

http://ccw.acu.edu

Magazine about bringing the gospel onto the campus.

Chi Alpha

http://avalon.syr.edu:80/ChiAlpha/

Web page about Chi Alpha Christian Ministries, specifically on the campus of Syracuse University.

1 Corinthians 2:2 Home Page

http://www.cs.indiana.edu/hyplan/jstogdil.html

Home page serving several Christian groups, particularly focused toward high school and college students. Features include several youth groups and an online newsletter.

Cornerstone College Ministries

http://www-ksl.stanford.edu/people/neller/cstone.html

Page sponsored by Menlo Park Presbyterian Church College Ministries in California.

HopeNet Web Page

http://www.crimson.com/hope

HopeWeb is a page containing information about the various Christian campus ministries located on the University of Texas at Austin. Also contains pointers to other online Christian resources.

ICCF Home Page

http://www.crhc.uiuc.edu/~mhsiao/iccf.html

Web page about the Illini Chinese Christian Fellowship at the University of Illinois, Urbana-Champaign. Group information, a searchable library, and pointers to other Christian resources can be found here.

InterVarsity Christian Fellowship

http://osnome.che.wisc.edu/~epperly/IVCF.html

Information about InterVarsity Christian Fellowship, an interdenominational ministry focusing on the college campus. Documents outline the history, practice, vision, and doctrinal basis of InterVarsity.

IVCF-L
listserv@uvbm.cc.buffalo.edu
Send a one line message text (not subject line)
that says:
subscribe ivcf-l Chris Christian
Group for the discussion of issues related to
InterVarsity Christian Fellowship, an interdenominational campus ministry.

Methodist-Anglican Society
http://www.york.ac.uk/~socs161/
University of York Christian society to help
believers deepen their understanding of God
and apply their faith in their daily lives.

MIT United Christian Residence/Orientation
http://www.mit.edu:8001/afs/athena/
activity/c/christro/www/home.html
Web page of Christian student groups at MIT.
Contains information about outreach, prayer,
and campus publicity.

Ohio University
linus.cs.ohiou.edu
(USA—Ohio.—Ohio University)
Student Organizations—The Bridge

The Scrawl
scrawl@vax.dickinson.edu
Send a request to the above address with your
name and e-mail address requesting a subscription to *The Scrawl*.
An online Christian newsletter written and
published by college students. Contents include
poetry, prayers, editorials, and other student-
oriented information.

Catholic

The American University
listserv.american.edu
(USA—Washington D.C.—The American
University)
Catholic Files

bit.listserv.catholic
Newsgroup version of the Catholic mailing
list.

Catholic
listserv@american.edu
Send a one line message text (not subject line)
that says:
subscribe catholic Chris Christian

Discussion group for Catholics interested in
discussing their discipleship to Jesus Christ in
terms of the Catholic approach to Christianity.
Not for attacks on Catholicism.

Catholic-Action
rfreeman@vpnet.chi.il.us
Discussion of Catholic evangelism, church renewal, and the preservation of the traditions,
teachings, and values of the Catholic church.

Catholic Doctrine
catholic-request@sarto.gaithersburg.
md.us
Discussion of orthodox Catholic theology.
Not for attacks on Catholicism.

Catholic Resources on the Net
http://www.cs.cmu.edu:8001/Web/People/
spok/catholic.html
This Web page is designed to provide a central
index to Catholic information on the Internet.
Pointer topics include Latin masses, Bibles,
writings of the early church, Vatican II documents, encyclicals organized by Pope, and Catholic-related electronic books.

Catholic Spirituality
listserv@american.edu
Send a one line message text (not subject line)
that says:
subscribe spirit-l Chris Christian
Forum on spirituality in secular life in the context of the Roman Catholic faith.

Jesuits and the Sciences
http://www.luc.edu/~scilib/jessci.html
Information about the Society of Jesus and its
role in the sciences between 1600 and 1800.

Religion in England
http://www.iris.brown.edu/iris/RIE/
Religion_OV.html
An overview of England's religious traditions
with particular emphasis on the Church of England and the Roman Catholic Church. However, additional information about the Bible,
Protestant denominations, and non-Christian
religions are also online.

University of Toronto
gopher.utoronto.ca
(North America—Canada—University of
Toronto)

Other Information Providers at U of T—Computing in the Humanities—Other Academic Resources by Discipline—Religious Studies and Theology—Resources for Theological Studies

Vatican Exhibit
http://sunsite.unc.edu/expo/
vatican.exhibit/Vatican.exhibit.html
Online version of the Library of Congress Vatican exhibit. It is divided into several "rooms" including a Vatican Library, mathematics, music, and nature. Photographs, historical documents, brief biographies, and commentary populate this Web server.

Cell Church

Cell Church Discussion Group
listserv@bible.acu.edu
Send a one line message text (not subject line) that says:
subscribe cell-church
A discussion group for Christians interested in the cell church model of church life.

Cell Church Discussion Group Files
http://hal.cs.uiuc.edu/~jreid/cell-church/
Web page correlating to the cell church mailing list.

Christian Living

AgapeNet
agape@agape.org
Send a one line message text (not subject line) that says:
subscribe agape.net
A discussion group for Christian fellowship.

alt.christnet
alt.christnet.christianlife
Unmoderated discussion groups covering various aspects of the Christian life.

Areopagus
http://www.catalog.com/lionsden/areo/
index.html
Christian electronic magazine dealing with opinions and issues related to faith.

bit.listserv.christia
Newsgroup version of the Christian mailing list.

Brother Mark's Christian Material
http://www.tit.fi/~mark/xian_1.html
Resources related to revival and Christian living. Also contains pointers to other resources. Cute section on the lighter side of Christianity.

Center for the Advancement of Paleo Orthodoxy
http://www.usit.net/public/CAPO/
capohome.html
Home page for CAPO, a biblical and historic consortium with the purpose of bringing ancient biblical light to modern issues.

Christia
listserv@asuvm.inre.asu.edu
Send a one line message text (not subject line) that says:
subscribe christia Chris Christian
A discussion group on the practical Christian life.

Christia Library
http://www.ihi.aber.ac.uk/~spk/
christia.html
Web page containing essays on the practical Christian life, in affiliation with the Christia mailing list.

Christianity
http://www.cs.colorado.edu/homes/mcbryan/
public_html/bb/27/summary.html
Page focused on Christianity and the Christian life.

Edinburgh Christian WWW Server
http://www.dcs.ed.ac.uk/misc/local/ecwww/
A Christian Web page complete with humor, evangelistic tracts, and electronic books. A love letter from Jesus, a collection of Bible quiz questions, Charles Spurgeon's *The Throne of Grace*, and articles including "Christ the Uncaged Lion" and "The Importance of Jesus Christ in My Life."

Focus on the Family Newsletter
listserv@netcentral.net
Send a one line message text (not subject line) that says:
subscribe fof-list Chris Christian
An unofficial distribution of Dr. James Dobson's monthly Focus on the Family newsletters.

Icthus
bluejack@omni.voicenet.com

Not a discussion group. Monthly journal devoted to the discussion of the great questions of our age.

Mail-JC
MAILJC-REQUEST@GRIAN.CPS.ALTADENA.CA.US
Send a one line message text (not subject line) that says:
subscribe mailjc Chris Christian
A friendly discussion group for Christians. Debates between Christians and non-Christians are not appropriate for this group.

No Fear
http://rgfn.epcc.edu:8001/users/ab939/no.fear.html
An online Christian magazine written from the perspective of an apostolic, pentecostal body.

The Scrawl
scrawl@vax.dickinson.edu
Send a request to the above address with your name and e-mail address requesting a subscription to *The Scrawl*.
An online Christian newsletter written and published by college students. Contents include poetry, prayers, editorials, and other student-oriented information.

soc.religion.christian
Moderated discussion about all aspects of the Christian faith. Topics include, but are not limited to: eschatology, worship, denominations, soteriology, evangelism, churches, and Christian culture.

Christianity, General

alt.religion.christian
Unmoderated newsgroup about all facets of Christianity.

Christianity
http://www.cs.colorado.edu/homes/mcbryan/public_html/bb/27/summary.html
Page focused on Christianity and the Christian life.

Regent University
beacon.regent.edu
(USA—Virginia—Regent)
Academic Departments—School of Divinity

soc.religion.christian
Moderated discussion about all aspects of the Christian faith. Topics include, but are not limited to: eschatology, worship, denominations, soteriology, evangelism, churches, and Christian culture.

Church

alt.org.royal-rangers
Unmoderated newsgroup about the Royal Rangers, an Assemblies of God youth program.

Cell Church Discussion Group
listserv@bible.acu.edu
Send a one line message text (not subject line) that says:
subscribe cell-church
A discussion group for Christians interested in the cell church model of church life.

Cell Church Discussion Group Files
http://hal.cs.uiuc.edu/~jreid/cell-church/
Web page correlating to the cell church mailing list.

Church Planters
listserv@bible.acu.edu
Send a one line message text (not subject line) that says:
subscribe churchplanters
A discussion group for Christians interested in historical and present-day church planters.

Cornerstone College Ministries
http://www-ksl.stanford.edu/people/neller/cstone.html
Page sponsored by Menlo Park Presbyterian Church College Ministries in California.

Soc.Religion.Christian.Youth-Work
youth-work@ucs.orst.edu
Send a one line message text (not subject line) that says:
subscribe christian@church.org
to the above address and put your Internet address in place of christian@church.org.
E-mail version of the soc.religion.christian.youth-work USENET group. If you subscribe to this list, you will receive everything posted to the newsgroup.

soc.religion.christian.youth-work

Moderated discussion about ministry to young people. Christians involved in youth work are encouraged to share stories, struggles, prayer requests, resources, suggestions, and anything else that could assist another in that ministry.

Soc.Religion.Christian.Youth-Work Web Page

http://www.engr.orst.edu:80/~freilish/youth-work.html

A Web site associated with the soc.religion.christian.youth-work newsgroup. It features ideas for activities, Bible studies, and missions work and provides a place for prayer requests and announcements.

Xenos Christian Fellowship

http://www.Xenos.Org/Churches/Xenos/index.html

Independent church in Columbus, Ohio, with a focus on small group/home group ministry. Papers and ministry information are included.

Colleges

American Universities

http://www.clas.ufl.edu/CLAS/american-universities.html

List of United States colleges and universities with Web pages.

Bethel College

http://www.bethel.edu

Calvin College

http://www.calvin.edu

Cedarville College

http://www.cedarville.edu

Christian Colleges and Organizations

http://www.iclnet.org/pub/resources/christian-directory.txt

A directory of Christian colleges and organizations on the Internet.

Luther Seminary

http://www.luthersem.edu/home/

Messiah College

http://www.messiah.edu:5080/

Mississippi College

http://www.nnc.edu

Northwest Nazarene College

http://www.nnc.edu

Regent University

http://beacon.regent.edu

Seattle Pacific University

http://www.spu.edu

St. Olaf College

http://www.stolaf.edu

Wheaton College

http://www.wheaton.edu

Computers

Christian Communications Toolkit

listserv@bible.acu.edu

Send a one line message text (not subject line) that says:

subscribe ctt Chris Christian

Discussion and information about the use of computer technology in ministry.

Christian Consortium Network

http://www.cs.odu.edu/~eisen_j

A Web page that describes the Christian Consortium Network. CCN is an attempt to create a virtual Christian community within cyberspace that includes everything from a school to a chapel. Information includes CCN's philosophy, plans, and works in progress.

Cross Connect

http://www.xc.org/xc.html

Membership association committed to bridging the gap between the Christian community and state-of-the-art electronic communications.

GodlyGraphics

majordomo@cybernetics.net

Send a one line message text (not subject line) that says:

subscribe gg-list

Discussion of Christian uses of computer graphics and animation. Trading of ideas, objects, and joint projects are encouraged.

Logos Research Systems

http://islander.whidbey.net/~logos/

Web page sponsored by Logos Research Systems, a developer of computerized Bible software.

Morning Star Technical Services
http://www.MorningStar.org
Information about the use of computers in worldwide missionary work. Details about a Christian electronic publishing project.

Rice University
riceinfo.rice.edu
(USA—Texas—Rice University)
Information by Subject Area—Religion and Philosophy

ShareNet Tech
hub@xc.org
Send a one line message text (not subject line) that says:
subscribe tech Chris Christian
Discussion of the use of technology in missions.

Tictalk
listserv@bible.acu.edu
Send a one line message text (not subject line) that says:
subscribe tictalk Chris Christian
Technology in the Church discussion.

Contemporary Christian Music

Alive 93–5 Christian CD Library Database
alive935@mc.edu
Send a one line message text (not subject line) that says:
help
A database of Contemporary Christian Music songs, albums, and artists that can be searched via e-mail. Searches can be done on key words in song titles, album titles, and artist names. By sending the aforementioned help request, you will receive information about querying the database.

alt.music.amy-grant
FAQs: Amy Grant FAQ
An unmoderated discussion of Amy Grant and her music.

Amy Grant—The Archive
http://www.ipc.uni-tuebingen.de/art/art.html
Information about Amy Grant.

Canadian CCM Current Page
http://www.io.org/~djcl/cccp.html
Contemporary Christian Music information from a Canadian perspective.

Charlie Peacock
listserv@netcentral.net
Send a one line message text (not subject line) that says:
subscribe peacock-list Chris Christian
Discussion about the CCM artist Charlie Peacock.

Christian Artists Web Pages
http://linus.cs.ohiou.edu/~wlhd/alight/cartists.html
Web page with pointers to various Christian musician WWW pages.

Christian Music
listserv@netcentral.net
Send a one line message text (not subject line) that says:
subscribe christian-music-list Chris Christian
The latest information about people and events in the Christian music field.

Christian Music Online
http://www.cmo.com/cmo/index.html
Contemporary Christian Music page with top songs, artist profiles, and ordering information.

Christian Musicians Page
http://www.umich.edu/~mozzer/christian/cmusic.html
Pointers to Web sites about Christian musicians.

Contemporary Christian Music Pictures
http://csclub.uwaterloo.ca/u/gjhurlbu/ccm.html
Digitized photographs of Contemporary Christian Musicians using the GIF format.

Contemporary Christian Music Site
http://www.acs.psu.edu/users/jws/ccmpage.html
Web page dedicated to Contemporary Christian Music brought to you by the TLeM folks.

Contemporary Christian Music SIG
http://www.ncf.carleton.ca/freeport/sigs/arts/music/christian/menu
Web page about Contemporary Christian Music sponsored by the National Capital FreeNet.

E-Text Archives
gopher.etext.org
Zines-by-subject—Religious

Friends of Amy Grant
listserv@netcentral.net
Send a one line message text (not subject line) that says:
subscribe amy-list Chris Christian
A one-way distribution list of newsworthy items for the official Amy Grant fan club, Friends of Amy.

Guitar Music Archives
http://www.coe.uncc.edu:80/~cmpilato/music/ccm_guitar.html
Find guitar chords to Christian songs using the World Wide Web.

The Lighthouse Electronic Magazine
listserv@netcentral.net
Send a one line message text (not subject line) that says:
subscribe lighthouse-list Chris Christian
The Lighthouse Electronic Magazine is a monthly electronic magazine that focuses on various forms of contemporary Christian music (CCM). It includes artist interviews, album reviews, and other articles about the ministry of Christian music.

The Lighthouse Electronic Magazine Web
http://www.netcentral.net/lighthouse/index.html
Web edition of TLeM, complete with photos, graphics, and more.

LineNoise
http://www.catalog.com/lionsden/linenoise/index.html
Electronic magazine about alternative contemporary Christian music.

Marathon Records
http://www.zilker.net:80/netads/arts/music/marathon/
Collection of independent alternative Christian bands including Farewell to Juliet and Able Cain.

Margaret Becker
http://www.cs.iastate.edu/~anderson/mb.html
Unofficial Margaret Becker Web page consisting of a discography, video information, re-

printed articles from CCM Magazine, tour information, and sound clips.

Mississippi College
gopher.mc.edu
(USA—Mississippi—Mississippi College)
Alive 93–5 WHJT Catalog of Contemporary Christian Music.

Netcentral
http://www.netcentral.net
Home of numerous officially-sponsored Christian music sites including Charlie Peacock, Reunion Records, Benson Music Group, Gospel Music Association, and more.

rec.music.christian
FAQs: Christian Radio Station List FAQ
Rec.Music.Christian Newsgroup FAQ
Worship Song FAQ
Amy Grant FAQ
Discography of contemporary Christian musicians
Christian Wedding Songs
Christian Funeral Songs
Phil Keaggy Information Phile
Amy Grant Information List
Take 6 Discography
Country Christian FAQ
Unmoderated discussion about Contemporary Christian Music.

Rec.Music.Christian Home Page
http://www.pencom.com/subdirs/rmc/home.html
Web page associated with the rec.music.christian newsgroup. Contains pointers to the FAQs and other CCM-related information.

Sam Phillips Mailing List
t.bowden@qub.ac.uk
Send a one line message text (not subject line) that says:
subscribe sam
Discussion of the singer Sam Phillips.

Sam Phillips Web Page
http://boris.qub.ac.uk/tony/sam/intro.html
A home page all about Sam (formerly Leslie) Phillips, the singer who left the CCM industry and entered mainstream music. Biographical information, articles, and pictures highlight this site.

SOAE

listserv@music.acu.edu

Send a one line message text (not subject line) that says:

subscribe soae Chris Christian

Mailing list for the Screams of Abel electronic magazine, which focuses on alternative, thrash, metal, and other non-mainstream Christian music.

Steve Taylor Web Page

http://www.ncf.carleton.ca/freenet/
rootdir/menus/sigs/arts/music/
christian/artist/staylor.a

Unofficial Web page about Steve Taylor including biographical information, discography, videography, and various interesting tidbits.

Creation vs. Evolution

talk.origins

FAQs: Includes:
Talk.Origins Welcome FAQ
Age of Earth Debate FAQ
Reading List for Creationism and Evolution

A secular newsgroup discussing the origin of life. Lively and pointed debates about creation versus evolution and other topics. Good resource for additional information about the evolution debate, often from evolutionists.

Creeds

Christia Library

http://www.ihi.aber.ac.uk/~spk/
christia.html

Christian living, creeds, Christia library.

Lutheran Homepage

http://www.maths.tcd.ie/hyplan/thomas/
lutheran/page.html

Developed by a student with a focus on the Evangelical Lutheran Church in America and Lutheranism in general. References include *Luther's Small Catechism* and the Athanasian Creed as well as ELCA youth and general activities and information.

Christian Reformed Church

http://www.anes.rochester.edu/crc.html

Information for, by, and about the Christian Reformed Church in North America, including news releases, missions information, and creeds and confessions.

Cults

alt.support.ex-cult

Secular discussion and support group for ex-cult members; also question and answers about various cults.

Abilene Christian University

bible.acu.edu

(USA—Texas—College of Biblical and Family Studies, Abilene Christian University)
Bible and Theological Information

Christian Research Institute Journal Articles

file://iclnet93.iclnet.org/pub/resources/
text/cri/cri-jrnl/crijnl.html

Articles from the *CRI Journal* provided by the Institute for Christian Leadership.

Devotions

Charles Spurgeon's Morning and Evening Devotionals

http://www.cs.pitt.edu/~planting/books/
spurgeon/morn_eve/morn_eve.html

A Web page containing the *Morning and Evening* devotionals written by C. H. Spurgeon.

Online Today

http://unicks.calvin.edu/today.html

Daily devotional online.

Our Daily Bread

http://unicks.calvin.edu/daily-bread/

View the *Our Daily Bread* devotional. You can select recent dates by using the graphical calendar and previous months are available via the archive. Pointer to the Radio Bible Class page.

Proverbs

ronm@slc.slac.stanford.edu

Not a discussion group. Rather an opportunity to receive a few Proverbs mailed to you on a mostly daily basis.

Sunday Snippets

ab531@cfn.cs.dal.ca

Weekly publication of a biblical essay, quotation, or other devotional material on various topics.

Verse of the Day

Contact listserv@netcentral.net
Send a one line message text (not subject line) that says:

```
subscribe votd-list Chris Christian
```
Daily verse delivered to your e-mailbox.

Words of Hope
```
http://unicks.calvin.edu/woh
```
Online devotional.

Early Church

The American University
```
listserv.american.edu
```
(USA—Washington D.C.—The American University)
Catholic Files—Documents of the Roman Catholic Church—Writings of the Church Fathers

Augustine
```
listserv@ccat.sas.upenn.edu
```
Send a one line message text (not subject line) that says:
```
subscribe augustine Chris Christian
```
This is not a Christian group, but a scholarly discussion of the person and writings of Augustine, Bishop of Hippo.

Early Christian Thought and Literature (elenchus)
```
LISTSERV@ACADVM1.UOTTAWA.CA
```
Send a one line message text (not subject line) that says:
```
subscribe elenchus Chris Christian
```
A group devoted to discussing early Christian thought and literature. Topics include the development of the canon of Scripture, archaeology, exegesis, and theology during the time period between A.D. 100 and 500.

Guide to Early Church Documents
```
ftp://iclnet93.iclnet.org/pub/resources/
christian-history.html
```
Pointer page related to the early Christian church.

Memorial University of Newfoundland
```
cwis.ucs.mun.ca
```
(North America—Canada—Memorial University of Newfoundland)
MUN Campus Information—Academic Departments—Religious Studies—3900—Religious Resources and Texts—Religious Texts—Apostolic Fathers

University of Pennsylvania
```
gopher.upenn.edu
```
(USA—Pennsylvania—University of Pennsylvania)
Gopher Servers at Penn—Center for Computer Analysis of Texts—Archives of the Center for Computer Analysis of Texts—Religion—Church Writers

Ecumenical Dialog

Diftx-L
```
listserv@yalevm.cis.yale.edu
```
Send a one line message text (not subject line) that says:
```
subscribe diftx-l Chris Christian
```
A discussion group that allows thoughtful constructive dialogue between the many different varieties of Christianity that exist. These varieties include denominational, cultural, and theological differences.

Ecunet
```
helper@ecunet.org
```
Information by and about numerous denominations, much of it provided by the denominations themselves.

Evangelicals and Catholics Together
```
http://saturn.colorado.edu:8080/
Christian/EvangAndCath.html
```
Ecumenical document.

Education

The Art House
```
http://www.netcentral.net/
arthouse.index.html
```
Home page of the Art House, a non-profit organization dedicated to cultivating the Christian mind in the field of art.

AskERIC
```
http://eryx.syr.edu/COWSHome.html
```
Web center for the federally-funded Educational Resources Information Center. Not Christian, but significant resources for Christian educators are available.

Association of Christians Teaching Sociology
```
listserv@bible.acu.edu
```
Send a one line message text (not subject line) that says:
```
subscribe tictalk Chris Christian
```
Discussion among Christian sociology teachers.

Center for Biblical Literacy Online
http://www.cbl.org/cbl
A "virtual campus" created by the Center for Biblical Literacy's School of Theological Studies. CBL offers undergraduate and graduate programs in biblical studies through distance learning.

Educational Resources Information Center
ericir.syr.edu
Other education resources.

Christian Consortium Network
http://www.cs.odu.edu/~eisen_j
A Web page that describes the Christian Consortium Network. CCN is an attempt to create a virtual Christian community within cyberspace that includes everything from a school to a chapel. Information includes CCN's philosophy, plans, and works in progress.

Faith-Learning
mailserv@baylor.edu
Send a one line message text (not subject line) that says:
subscribe faith-learning Chris Christian
A discussion group for Christian educators seeking to encourage one another as they incorporate their faith into higher education. Topics include effective teaching, learning, scholarship, conference announcement, and suggestions on how to bring faith into the education system.

Presbyterian School of Christian Education
psce-request@ecunet.org
Send a one line message text (not subject line) that says:
subscribe psce Chris Christian
A discussion group about the Presbyterian School of Christian Education, a Presbyterian Church (U.S.A.) theological institution.

Regent University
beacon.regent.edu
(USA—Virginia—Regent)
Academic Departments—School of Education

St. Olaf College
gopher.stolaf.edu
(USA—Minnesota—St. Olaf College)
Internet Resources—St. Olaf Sponsored Mailing-Lists

Evangelism

Edinburgh Christian WWW Server
http://www.dcs.ed.ac.uk/misc/local/ecwww/
A Christian Web page complete with humor, evangelistic tracts, and electronic books. A love letter from Jesus, a collection of Bible quiz questions, Charles Spurgeon's *The Throne of Grace*, and articles including "Christ the Uncaged Lion" and "The Importance of Jesus Christ in My Life."

Questions and Answers about Religion and Christianity
http://www.ugcs.caltech.edu/~werdna/q&a/q&a.html#
A series of questions and answers about religion, and particularly Christianity, written and collected by a Christian who has asked them himself. In addition to his responses, there is opportunity to answer them for yourself.

What Is a Christian?
http://www.cs.indiana.edu/hyplan/ljray/gospel.html
Online tract.

Wheaton College
gopher.wheaton.edu
(USA—Illinois—Wheaton College)
Church—Christian Studies Information

Family

Family Research Council
http://www.balltown.cma.com/~ault/fof/misc/frc/frc.html
Unofficial Web page containing information and newsletters from Gary Bauer's Family Research Council.

Focus on the Family Newsletter Archive
http://www.iclnet.org/pub/resources/text/Focus.on.Family/fofn.html
Web page containing copies of Dr. James Dobson's monthly newsletters.

Promise Keepers
http://www.whitedove.com/PK/index.html
Unofficial Promise Keepers Web page.

Global Christianity

Global Christianity Discussion
listserv@qucdn.queensu.ca

Send a one line message text (not subject line) that says:

`subscribe globlx-1 Chris Christian`

Discussion of global Christianity.

UgandaNet
`listserv@bible.acu.edu`

Send a one line message text (not subject line) that says:

`subscribe ugandanet Chris Christian`

A network of and by Ugandans and friends of Uganda. Housed at Abilene Christian University.

World Christian Internet Resources
`http://www.morningstar.org/world-christian.html`

Internet resources for the global-thinking Christian.

History

Ecchst-L
`listserv@bgu.edu`

Send a one line message text (not subject line) that says:

`subscribe ecchst-1 Chris Christian`

Discussion list for the study of church history, history of Christianity, and historical theology.

Histec–2
`mailserv@baylor.edu`

Send a one line message text (not subject line) that says:

`subscribe histec–21 Chris Christian`

Discussion group for conversations, debate, and exchange of information concerning the history of evangelical Christianity.

Ioudaios-L
`listserv@lehigh.edu`

Send a one line message text (not subject line) that says:

`subscribe ioudaios-1 Chris Christian`

Not a Christian list but an electronic seminary devoted to first century Judaism. Of particular interest is its focus on Flavius Josephus and Philo Judaeus of Alexandria.

Rice University
`riceinfo.rice.edu`

(USA—Texas—Rice University)
Information by Subject Area—Religion and Philosophy

Scrolls from the Dead Sea
`http://sunsite.unc.edu/expo/deadsea.scrolls.exhibit/intro.html`

An online exhibit of the Dead Sea scrolls based on the Library of Congress exhibit. The online version includes pictures of the scrolls, historical information about the Qumran community, and articles about the scrolls.

University of Virginia, Special Collections
`gopher.lib.virginia.edu`

(USA—Virginia—UVA)
Subject Organization—Historical—Electronic Antiquity

Vanderbilt Divinity Special Collections
`vuinfo.vanderbilt.edu`

(USA—Tennessee—Vanderbilt)
Library Resources and Services—About Libraries at Vanderbilt University—Divinity Library

Vatican Exhibit
`http://sunsite.unc.edu/expo/vatican.exhibit/Vatican.exhibit.html`

Online version of the Library of Congress Vatican exhibit. It is divided into several "rooms" including a Vatican Library, mathematics, music, and nature. Photographs, historical documents, brief biographies, and commentary populate this Web server.

Homeschooling

alt.education.home-school.christian
Moderated alternative to misc.education.home-school.christian. Discussion of all aspects of Christian homeschooling.

Home-ed
`home-ed-request@mainstream.com`

Not specifically a Christian mailing list. A discussion list concerning the various aspects and methods of homeschooling.

Home-Ed-Politics
`home-ed-politics-request@ mainstream.com`

Not specifically a Christian mailing list. A discussion list concerning the political issues dealing with homeschooling.

Jon's Homeschool Resource Page
`http://www.armory.com:80/~jon/hs/HomeSchool.html`

Not a Christian page but rather a collection of pointers to USENET groups, Web pages, Gopher servers, and other resources appropriate to homeschooling.

misc.education.home-school.christian
Unmoderated group to discuss all aspects of Christian homeschooling.

misc.education.home-school.misc
FAQs: Home Ed Digest
Unmoderated secular group to discuss all aspects of homeschooling.

Humor

Brother Mark's Christian Material
http://www.tit.fi/~mark/xian_1.html
Resources related to revival and Christian living. Also contains pointers to other resources. Cute section on the lighter side of Christianity.

Edinburgh Christian WWW Server
http://www.dcs.ed.ac.uk/misc/local/ecwww/
A Christian Web page complete with humor, evangelistic tracts, and electronic books. A love letter from Jesus, a collection of Bible quiz questions, Charles Spurgeon's *The Throne of Grace*, and articles including "Christ the Uncaged Lion" and "The Importance of Jesus Christ in My Life."

Languages

B-Greek
majordomo@virginia.edu
Send a one line message text (not subject line) that says:
subscribe b-greek
Focused on the scholarly study of the New Testament in Greek. While anyone can subscribe, participants should have at least a basic proficiency in Greek. Sponsored by the Center for Christian Study, an independent Christian ministry at the University of Virginia.

B-Hebrew
majordomo@virginia.edu
Send a one line message text (not subject line) that says:
subscribe b-hebrew
Focused on the scholarly study of the Old Testament in Hebrew. While anyone can subscribe, participants should have at least a basic proficiency in Hebrew and Aramaic. Sponsored by the Center for Christian Study, an independent Christian ministry at the University of Virginia.

Basic English Commentaries Project
http://www.aiai.ed.ac.uk/~jkk/wycliffe-words.html
Information about a Wycliffe project to make Bible commentaries available to third-world pastors in their own languages using volunteers with computers.

Durham University
delphi.dur.ac.uk
(Europe—United Kingdom—Durham University Information Service)
Academic Departments and Faculties—Departments Listed P-T—Theology—Durham Centre for Theological Research—Theology and Computers—Software for Theologians: A Selection—Greek & Hebrew Font and Word Processing Software

SIL Associates
sil-assoc@cogsci.ed.ac.uk
Information about Summer Institute of Linguistics, a sister ministry to Wycliffe Bible Translators.

University of Pennsylvania
gopher.upenn.edu
(USA—Pennsylvania—University of Pennsylvania)
Gopher Servers at Penn—Center for Computer Analysis of Texts—Archives of the Center for Computer Analysis of Texts—Religion—Biblical

Vanderbilt Divinity Special Collections
vuinfo.vanderbilt.edu
(USA—Tennessee—Vanderbilt)
Library Resources and Services—About Libraries at Vanderbilt University—Divinity Library

Leadership

Institute for Christian Leadership
http://www.iclnet.org/
Web pages sponsored by the Institute for Christian Leadership, with information and resources for Christian leaders and educators.

Leadership
majordomo@iclnet93.iclnet.org

Send a one line message text (not subject line) that says:

subscribe leadership

Discussion group geared toward Christian leaders intended to provide opportunity to share ministry ideas and work through problems.

Libraries

Emory University, Pitts Theology Library
http://www.pitts.emory.edu/ptl_home.html

A Web server providing access to the online card catalog, reference materials, archives, manuscripts, and pointers to other libaries.

Library of Congress
marvel.loc.gov

(USA—Washington D.C.—Library of Congress)

Presbyterian College
gopher.presby.edu

(USA—South Carolina—Presbyterian College)

Library Resources—Other On-line Library Catalogs

Yale University
yaleinfo.yale.edu

(USA—Connecticut—Yale University)

Browse Yaleinfo—Library Catalogs World-Wide

Literature

Christlit
listserv@bethel.edu

Send a one line message text (not subject line) that says:

subscribe christlit Chris Christian

Discussion group focusing on the relationship between Christianity and literature. Not for disputes about theology.

C. S. Lewis Page
http://sleepy.usu.edu/~slq9v/cslewis/index.html

A Web page about the noted author C. S. Lewis. Includes information about his life and his work.

E-Text Archives
gopher.etext.org

Gutenberg.

Gutenberg E-Text Web Page
http://med-amsa.bu.edu/Gutenberg/Welcome.html

A project to make books freely available in an electronic format. The eclectic mix of titles ranges from *Peter Pan* to the *CIA World Factbook*; Christian titles include the King James Bible and works by G. K. Chesterton.

Early Christian Thought and Literature (elenchus)
LISTSERV@ACADVM1.UOTTAWA.CA

Send a one line message text (not subject line) that says:

subscribe elenchus Chris Christian

A group devoted to discussing early Christian thought and literature. Topics include the development of the canon of Scripture, archaeology, exegesis, and theology during the time period between A.D. 100 and 500.

Pointing the Way: A Guide to Christian Literature on the Internet
http://www.calvin.edu/pw.html

A Web page developed by the Not Just Bibles team in coordination with the Institute for Christian Leadership. The page is designed to provide a central directory to Christian Literature. Pointers include a variety of Bible translations, books, articles, and various creeds and confessions.

Liturgy

Durham University
delphi.dur.ac.uk

(Europe—United Kingdom—Durham University Information Service)

Academic Departments and Faculties—Departments Listed P-T—Theology—Durham Centre for Theological Research—Theology and Computers—Liturgical Texts on the Internet

University of Toronto
gopher.utoronto.ca

(North America—Canada—University of Toronto)

Other Information Providers at U of T—Computing in the Humanities—Other Academic Resources by Discipline—Religious Studies and Theology—Resources for Theological Studies

Leitourgia Home Page
http://www.liturgy.nd.edu/
   An effort sponsored by the Notre Dame Center for Pastoral Liturgy to provide an interactive multimedia base of information for those concerned with liturgy.

Lutheran

Concordia College
gopher.cord.edu
   (USA—Minnesota—Concordia College)
   The Church—Lutheran Vespers Sermons

Concordia University
crf.cuis.edu
   (USA—Illinois—Concordia University)
   Concordia University System—Each School of the Concordia University System—Concordia Theological Seminary—Library—The Lutheran Library of Electronic Texts and Information Resources

Gustavus Adolphus College
http://www.gac.edu
   Lutheran Information

Lutheran Homepage
http://www.maths.tcd.ie/hyplan/thomas/
   lutheran/page.html
   Developed by a student with a focus on the Evangelical Lutheran Church in America and Lutheranism in general. References include *Luther's Small Catechism* and the Athanasian Creed as well as ELCA youth and general activities and information.

Luthhour
mailserv@crf.cuis.edu
subscribe luthhour
   Sermons from the Lutheran Hour radio program delivered to your desktop.

Memorial University of Newfoundland
cwis.ucs.mun.ca
   (North America—Canada—Memorial University of Newfoundland)
   MUN Campus Information—Academic Departments—Religious Studies—3900—Religious Resources and Texts—Religious Texts—Martin Luther

University of Illinois at Chicago
gopher.uic.edu

(USA—Illinois—University of Illinois at Chicago)
   The Researcher—History—H-Net—H-German—Project Wittenberg (Lutheran History)

University of Toronto
gopher.utoronto.ca
   (North America—Canada—University of Toronto)
   Other Information Providers at U of T—Computing in the Humanities—Other Academic Resources by Discipline—Religious Studies and Theology—Resources for Theological Studies

Wittenburg
mailserv@crf.cuis.edu
   Leave the subject line blank and send a one line message that says:
subscribe wittenberg
   A discussion group on the topic of Lutheran Church history.

Mennonite

Christian Peacemaker Teams Network
listserv@uci.com
   Send a one line message text (not subject line) that says:
subscribe cptnet Chris Christian
   Discussion among Christians working for justice and peace sponsored by the Mennonite church and Church of the Brethren.

Menno
listserv@uci.com
   Send a one line message text (not subject line) that says:
subscribe menno Chris Christian
   Discussion group focusing on the Anabaptist/Mennonite faith. Topics include doctrine, traditions, simple living, and pacifism.

Messianic

alt.messianic
   Unmoderated discussion by and about Messianic Jews and Jewish-Christian discussions.

Methodist

Auburn Wesley Foundation
http://www.eng.auburn.edu/users/jasonc/
   wesleyhome.html

Page for the Wesley Foundation at Auburn University.

Memorial University of Newfoundland
cwis.ucs.mun.ca

(North America—Canada—Memorial University of Newfoundland)

MUN Campus Information—Academic Departments—Religious Studies—3900—Religious Resources and Texts—Religious Texts—John Wesley

Methodist-Anglican Society
http://www.york.ac.uk/~socs161/

University of York Christian society to help believers deepen their understanding of God and apply their faith in their daily lives.

Missions

Abilene Christian University
bible.acu.edu

(USA—Texas—College of Biblical and Family Studies, Abilene Christian University)

Missions Information

Basic English Commentaries Project
http://www.aiai.ed.ac.uk/~jkk/wycliffe-words.html

Information about a Wycliffe project to make Bible commentaries available to third-world pastors in their own languages using volunteers with computers.

Church Planters
listserv@bible.acu.edu

Send a one line message text (not subject line) that says:

subscribe churchplanters

A discussion group for Christians interested in historical and present-day church planters.

Croatian Academic and Research Network
rujan.srce.hr

English Language—Information, Various Institutions and Projects—Christian Information Service

DELTA Ministries
http://www.teleport.com/~pmagee/delta.html

Information about DELTA Ministries International, an organization specializing in short-term mission work.

MissionNet
majordomo@iclnet93.iclnet.org

Send a one line message text (not subject line) that says:

subscribe missionnet Chris Christian

Discussion groups for missions. Topics include mission opportunities, biographies, organizations, and other mission-related issues.

MKNet
mknet-request@calvin.edu

Send a one line subject line that says: "subscribe" (without the quotes).

Mailing list for Missionary Kids (MKs) and those interested in MKs to encourage one another and share in the unique struggles of being an MK.

MKNet
http://www.calvin.edu/~heknat/mknet/mknet.html

Web page for Missionary kids.

Morning Star Technical Services
http://www.MorningStar.org

Information about the use of computers in worldwide missionary work. Details about a Christian electronic publishing project.

ShareNet Misc
hub@xc.org

Send a one line message text (not subject line) that says:

subscribe misc Chris Christian

Missions information.

SIL Associates
sil-assoc@cogsci.ed.ac.uk

Information about Summer Institute of Linguistics, a sister ministry to Wycliffe Bible Translators.

Speed the Need
mailserv@crf.cuis.edu

Send a one line message text (not subject line) that says:

subscribe stn

Speed the Need serves as a way to send out news flashes concerning the needs of foreign Christian missionaries.

Teen Mania
http://www.ksu.edu/~airforc/tmpix.html

Web page about Teen Mania missions organization. Information about conferences and mission trips are available.

UgandaNet
listserv@bible.acu.edu
    Send a one line message text (not subject line)
that says:
subscribe ugandanet Chris Christian
    A network of and by Ugandans and friends of
Uganda. Housed at Abilene Christian University.

Youth with a Mission International
http://www.xs4all.nl:80/~gwb/YWAM/
    Web page introducing YWAM and their mis-
sions activities.

Music

The Catholic University of America
vmsgopher.cua.edu
    (USA—Washington, D.C.—The Catholic
University of America)
    Special Resources—Database of Gregorian
Chants

Choralist
listproc@lists.colorado.edu
subscribe choralist Chris Christian
    Not specifically a Christian mailing list. Dis-
cussion of topics related to choral music including composers, techniques, problems, and ideas
relevant to college, public school, and church
choral directors.

Christian Music
listserv@netcentral.net
    Send a one line message text (not subject line)
that says:
subscribe christian-music-list Chris
Christian
    The latest information about people and
events in the Christian music field.

Christian Music Online
http://www.cmo.com/cmo/index.html
    Contemporary Christian Music page with top
songs, artist profiles, and ordering information.

Guitar Music Archives
http://www.coe.uncc.edu:80/~cmpilato/
    music/ccm_guitar.html
    Find guitar chords to Christian songs using
the World Wide Web.

The Lighthouse Electronic Magazine
listserv@netcentral.net
    Send a one line message text (not subject line)
that says:
subscribe lighthouse-list Chris Christian
    The Lighthouse Electronic Magazine is a
monthly electronic magazine that focuses on
various forms of contemporary Christian music
(CCM). It includes artist interviews, album reviews, and other articles about the ministry of
Christian music.

The Lighthouse Electronic Magazine Web
http://www.netcentral.net/lighthouse/
    index.html
    Web edition of TLeM, complete with photos,
graphics, and more.

Netcentral
http://www.netcentral.net
    Home of numerous officially-sponsored
Christian music sites including Charlie Peacock, Reunion Records, Benson Music Group,
Gospel Music Association, and more.

Praise Songs
http://www.crhc.uiuc.edu/~mhsiao/iccf/
    songFile.html
    Collection of Christian praise songs with lyrics
and guitar chords.

Organizations

Bethany Christian Services
gopher.bethany.org
    About Bethany Christian Services.

Bethany Christian Services
http://www.bethany.org/
    Introduction to Bethany Christian Services.

Chi Alpha
http://avalon.syr.edu:80/ChiAlpha/
    Web page about Chi Alpha Christian Minis-
tries, specifically on the campus of Syracuse
University.

Cross Connect
http://www.xc.org/xc.html
    Membership association committed to bridg-
ing the gap between the Christian community
and state-of-the-art electronic communications.

Dance for Christ
http://jesus.ox.ac.uk/~rmedcalf/dfc1.html

A Christian arts group based in England that communicates the Christian faith using dance, mime, and movement.

DELTA Ministries
http://www.teleport.com/~pmagee/
delta.html

Information about DELTA Ministries International, an organization specializing in short-term mission work.

Evangelicals for Social Action
listserv@netcom.com

Send a one line message text (not subject line) that says:

subscribe esa christian@church.org

to the above address and put your Internet address in place of christian@church.org.

Mailing list for Evangelicals for Social Action, a non-profit organization dedicated to promote the integration faith, evangelism, and social action.

FreeWay Express
http://www.intele.net/~bowserd/
freeway.html

An online newsletter from a chapter within the Christian Motorcyclists Association.

Institute for Christian Leadership
http://www.iclnet.org/

Web pages sponsored by the Institute for Christian Leadership, with information and resources for Christian leaders and educators.

Jews for Jesus
http://www.jews-for-jesus.org

Web page associated with Jews for Jesus with information about the organization, evangelistic tips, and other resources.

Koinonia House
http://www.khouse.org/khouse/index.html

Koinonia House is a publishing ministry oriented toward the development of materials to improve the study and application of Scripture.

Morning Star Technical Services
http://www.MorningStar.org

Information about the use of computers in worldwide missionary work. Details about a Christian electronic publishing project.

Royal Rangers
alt.org.royal-rangers

Unmoderated newsgroup about the Royal Rangers, an Assemblies of God youth program.

Royal Rangers Web Page
http://www.rahul.net/rangers/

A home page associated with the Royal Rangers, a world-wide ministry to reach boys for Christ started by the Assemblies of God Church. Information about the ministry and how to join is found here.

Scargill House
http://www.mcc.ac.uk/~john/Scargill.html

Web about the Scargill House, a Christian conference and holiday center in England.

Springs of Life
http://emall.com/Springs/SOL1.html

An online Christian store that contains books, videos, clothing, and other products.

Orthodox

The Coptic Orthodox Church of Egypt
http://cs-www.bu.edu/faculty/best/pub/cn/
Home.html

Historical and cultural information about the Coptic Orthodox Church. Numerous biographies, articles, and creeds relevant to the Coptic tradition are included.

Eastern Orthodox Christianity
listserv@qucdn.queensu.ca

Send a one line message text (not subject line) that says:

subscribe eochr-1 Chris Christian

Discussion of the Eastern Orthodox Church.

Orthodox
listserv@iubvm.ucs.indiana.edu

Send a one line message text (not subject line) that says:

subscribe orthodox Chris Christian

Discussion group for the thoughtful exchange of information regarding Orthodox Christianity worldwide, with a particular emphasis on its role in and around Russia.

The Orthodox Christian Page
http://nikon.ssl.berkeley.edu:80/~dv/
orthodox/Orthodox.html

Web page about the Orthodox Church.

Pastors

Pastors Network
`mail-server@rhesys.mb.ca`
Send a one line message text (not subject line) that says:
`subscribe pasnet-l christian@church.org`
to the above address and put your Internet address in place of `christian@church.org`.
For discussion among pastors.

Politics

Conchr-L
`listserv@vm.temple.edu`
Send a one line message text (not subject line) that says:
`subscribe conchr-l Chris Christian`
Discussion group for conservative Christians. Topics include contemporary conservative perspectives on issues such as politics and economics.

Evangelicals for Social Action
`listserv@netcom.com`
Send a one line message text (not subject line) that says:
`subscribe esa christian@church.org`
to the above address and put your Internet address in place of `christian@church.org`.
Mailing list for Evangelicals for Social Action, a non-profit organization dedicated to promote the integration faith, evangelism, and social action.

Family Research Council Newsletter
`listserv@netcentral.net`
Send a one line message text (not subject line) that says:
`subscribe frc-list Chris Christian`
An unofficial distribution of Gary Bauer's monthly Family Research Council newsletters.

Home-Ed-Politics
`home-ed-politics-request@mainstream.com`
Not specifically a Christian mailing list. A discussion list concerning the political issues dealing with homeschooling.

Prayer

Prayer-L
`listserv@gitvm1.gatech.edu`
Send a one line message text (not subject line) that says:
`subscribe prayer-l Chris Christian`
Mailing list for prayer requests.

Prayer Network
`schuetsj@cnsvax.uwec.edu`
Network of prayer partners.

Presbyterian

Calvin-L
`listserv@listserv.ucalgary.ca`
Send a one line message text (not subject line) that says:
`subscribe calvin-l Chris Christian`
Discussion topics related to Calvinism.

Presbyterian College
`gopher.presby.edu`
(USA—South Carolina—Presbyterian College)
Religion Resources.

Presbyterian School of Christian Education
`psce-request@ecunet.org`
Send a one line message text (not subject line) that says:
`subscribe psce Chris Christian`
A discussion group about the Presbyterian School of Christian Education, a Presbyterian Church (U.S.A.) theological institution.

Pro-Life

Bethany Christian Services
`gopher.bethany.org`
What We Do—Nationwide—Adoption Services

Bethany Christian Services
`http://www.bethany.org/`
Introduction to Bethany Christian Services.

College Right to Life Connection
`listserv@netcentral.net`
Send a one line message text (not subject line) that says:
`subscribe crlc-list Chris Christian`
Pro-life information and discussion for and by college pro-life groups.

D.C. Metro Prolife News/Events Line
`http://www.clark.net/pub/jeffd/plnel.html`

A home page in support of D.C. Metro Prolife News/Events line, which provides pro-life news and information to people in the Washington, D.C., area. It includes the latest transcript of the News/Events line and pointers to other pro-life resources.

LifeLinks
http://www.cs.indiana.edu/hyplan/ljray/
lifelink.html

A Web page that contains pointers to pro-life information and resources on the Internet. Although it is run by a Christian, its intent is to provide a central repository of pro-life resources, regardless of their religious or political affiliation.

Pro-Life Infonet
listserv@netcentral.net

Send a one line message text (not subject line) that says:

subscribe infonet-list Chris Christian

Pro-life information and news flashes.

Pro-Life News
listserv@netcentral.net

Send a one line message text (not subject line) that says:

subscribe plnews-list Chris Christian

Pro-life newsletter.

The Pro-Life News
http://www.pitt.edu/~stfst/pln/
AboutPLN.html

Web page associated with The Pro-Life News electronic magazine. Current and archive volumes are accessible as well as archives of the Internet Pro-Life Journal.

Pro-Life Resources
http://www.pitt.edu/~stfst/
PLresources.html
Resources for pro-lifers.

Reference

Calvin College
gopher.calvin.edu
(USA—Michigan—Calvin College)
Christian Resources

Calvin College GoWeb Server
http://www.calvin.edu

A home page developed by Calvin College that has pointers to information about the college as well as other online Christian resources.

Catholic Resources on the Net
http://www.cs.cmu.edu:8001/Web/People/
spok/catholic.html

This Web page is designed to provide a central index to Catholic information on the Internet. Pointer topics include Latin masses, Bibles, writings of the early church, Vatican II documents, encyclicals organized by Pope, and Catholic-related electronic books.

The Christian Connection
http://www.amherst.edu:80/~drsharp/cc/

A site with numerous pointers to other online Christian resources.

Christian Cyberspace Companion
http://www.bakerbooks.com/ccc

A site designed to complement this book, including a current online version of the subject-oriented Christian Internet Directory (appendix C). Visit this site to find pointers to Christian materials, offer feedback for future editions of CCC, or correspond with the author.

Christian Resource List
http://saturn.colorado.edu:8080/
Christian/list.html

A Web page of pointers to Christian resources on the Internet including documents, newsgroups, Gopher servers, and other Web pages.

Christian Resources on the World Wide Web
http://hercules.geology.uiuc.edu/
~schimmri/christianity/christian.html

Pointers to a variety of Web pages of interest to the Christian community.

Christian White Pages
http://www.cs.odu.edu/~eisen_j/ccn/
list.html

A list of Christians on the Internet sponsored by the Christian Consortium Network.

Einet Galaxy Religion Page
http://galaxy.einet.net/galaxy/Arts-and-
Humanities/Religion.html

Page with pointers to various religious resources.

Guide to Early Church Documents
ftp://iclnet93.iclnet.org/pub/resources/
christian-history.html

Pointer page related to the early Christian church.

Not Just Bibles: A Guide to Christian Resources on the Internet
http://www.calvin.edu/Christian/
christian-resources.html
A Web page developed in association with the Institute for Christian Leadership. It contains a list of Christian resources including home pages, Gopher servers, USENET newsgroups, and mailing lists which relate to Classical Christianity.

Online Books Page
http://www.cs.cmu.edu:8001/Web/books.html
Front page for an index of hundreds of online books, including Christian and secular titles.

Pointing the Way: A Guide to Christian Literature on the Internet
http://www.calvin.edu/pw.html
A Web page developed by the Not Just Bibles team in coordination with the Institute for Christian Leadership. The page is designed to provide a central directory to Christian Literature. Pointers include a variety of Bible translations, books, articles, and various creeds and confessions.

University of Michigan
gopher.lib.umich.edu
(USA—Michigan—University of Michigan Libraries)
What's New and Featured Resources—Clearinghouse for Subject-Oriented Internet Resources Guides

Wheaton College
gopher.wheaton.edu
(USA—Illinois—Wheaton College)
Church—Christian Studies Information

Yahoo Christian Resources
http://akebono.stanford.edu/yahoo/
Society_and_Culture/Religion/
Christianity/
Pointers to many Christian resources

Reformed

Calvin College
gopher.calvin.edu
(USA—Michigan—Calvin College)

Christian Resources—The Christian Reformed Church

Christian Reformed Church
http://www.anes.rochester.edu/crc.html
Information for, by, and about the Christian Reformed Church in North America including news releases, missions information, and creeds and confessions.

CRC_Voices
crc-voices-request@calvin.edu
Send a one line message text (not subject line) that says:
subscribe crc-voices chris christian
A lively discussion group about doctrine, hermeneutics, theology, and other issues related to the Christian Reformed Church.

Religious Studies

ANDERE-L
listserv@ucsbvm.ucsb.ca
Send a one line message text (not subject line) that says:
sub andere-l Chris Christian
Secular discussion of theories, methods, and approaches to the study of religions. Membership is by application only and is limited to professors, graduate students, and other religious scholars.

Einet Galaxy Religion Page
http://galaxy.einet.net/galaxy/Arts-and-Humanities/Religion.html
Page with pointers to various religious resources.

Religious Studies Publications Journal
listserv@acadvm1.uottawa.ca
Send a one line message text (not subject line) that says:
subscribe contents Chris Christian
Journal of various religious studies.

Library of Congress
marvel.loc.gov
(USA—Washington D.C.—Library of Congress)
Global Electronic Library (By Subject)—Philosophy and Religion

Religion & Belief
http://nearnet.gnn.com/wic/
hum.toc.html#relig

Information about various religions found on the Internet.

`talk.religion.misc`
Discussions about religion.

University of Michigan
`gopher.lib.umich.edu`
(USA—Michigan—University of Michigan Libraries)
Humanities Resources—Philosophy and Religion

University of North Carolina Religious Texts
`calypso.oit.unc.edu`
(USA—North Carolina—UNC)
Worlds of SunSITE—Religious Texts

Revival

Brother Mark's Christian Material
`http://www.tit.fi/~mark/xian_1.html`
Resources related to revival and Christian living. Also contains pointers to other resources. Cute section on the lighter side of Christianity.

Ekklesia
`dzeigler@magnus.acs.ohio-state.edu`
Discussion group dealing with the Christian church and how to bring about renewal in it.

The Vineyard Archives
`http://groke.beckman.uiuc.edu/Vineyard/`
Information about the Toronto Vineyard experience.

Science

Science and Christianity
`schimmri@hercules.geology.uiuc.edu`
Include personal information about yourself (e.g. how you meet the subscription requirements shown below).
For Christians in the sciences to discuss relevant issues. To subscribe you must be (1) actively involved in physical or life sciences as a student, professor, or professional; (2) be a believing, practicing Christian; (3) civil in your contributions to the list.

`talk.origins`
FAQs: Includes:
Talk.Origins Welcome FAQ
Age of Earth Debate FAQ
Reading List for Creationism and Evolution

A secular newsgroup discussing the origin of life. Lively and pointed debates about creation versus evolution and other topics. Good resource for additional information about the evolution debate, often from evolutionists.

Seventh-Day Adventist

Andrews University
`gopher.andrews.edu`
(USA—Michigan—Andrews University)
Adventist Resources.

SDANet
`listserv@sdanet.org`
Send a one line message text (not subject line) that says:
`subscribe sdanet`
Open for discussion and questions regarding the Seventh-day Adventist church. Topics include theology, history, practice, and culture of Seventh-day Adventism.

SDAnet Gopher
`gopher.sdanet.org`
Seventh-day Adventist Information.

Theology

`alt.christnet.theology`
Unmoderated discussion group about Christian theology.

`alt.messianic`
Unmoderated discussion by and about Messianic Jews and Jewish-Christian discussions.

Calvin-L
`listserv@listserv.ucalgary.ca`
Send a one line message text (not subject line) that says:
`subscribe calvin-l Chris Christian`
Discussion topics related to Calvinism.

Catholic Doctrine
`catholic-request@sarto.gaithersburg.md.us`
Discussion of orthodox Catholic theology. Not for attacks on Catholicism.

Durham University
`delphi.dur.ac.uk`
(Europe—United Kingdom—Durham University Information Service)
Academic Departments and Faculties—Departments Listed P-T—Theology

Early Christian Thought and Literature (elenchus)
LISTSERV@ACADVM1.UOTTAWA.CA
Send a one line message text (not subject line) that says:
`subscribe elenchus Chris Christian`
A group devoted to discussing early Christian thought and literature. Topics include the development of the canon of Scripture, archaeology, exegesis, and theology during the time period between A.D. 100 and 500.

Ecotheol
mailbase@mailbase.ac.uk
Send a one line message text (not subject line) that says:
`subscribe ecotheol Chris Christian`
Discussion list for the study of ecological theology and ethics.

Emory University, Pitts Theology Library
http://www.pitts.emory.edu/ptl_home.html
A Web server providing access to the online card catalog, reference materials, archives, manuscripts, and pointers to other libaries.

Femrel-L
listserv@mizzou1.missouri.edu
Send a one line message text (not subject line) that says:
`subscribe femrel-1 Chris Christian`
Discussion of feminist theology, women and religion, and women's roles in the church.

Prophecy
prophecy@cyberearth.mscl.msstate.edu
Discussion of prophecy and the second coming.

Rice University
riceinfo.rice.edu
(USA—Texas—Rice University)
Information by Subject Area—Religion and Philosophy

Soc.Religion.Christian.Bible-Study Mail Server
listproc@spss.com
Send a one line message text (not subject line) that says:
`GET BIBLE filename`
to the above address and put the name of the FAQ in place of filename.
Mail server to distribute a variety of FAQs and studies pertinent to soc.religion.christian.bible-study. The following files are available:

Bible.List Information on Bible versions and their origins.

BibleStudy.Charter Charter of soc.religion.christian.bible-study.

E-Bible.FAQ Information relating to electronic Bibles.

Eschatology.1 A study in eschatology by Tom Albrecht.

Genealogies Discussion of genealogies in Matthew and Luke.

Genesis.Accounts Are the Genesis accounts in chronological order?

Genesis.Days How long were the days of creation?

Genesis.Gap Is there a gap between Genesis 1:1 and 1:2?

Genesis.Long_Days Defense of the day-age view.

Isaiah714 Commentary on the prophecy in Isaiah 7:14.

Judas.Death Harmonization of Mathew 27 and Acts 1 (the death of Judas).

Judas.Death.Crit Criticism of Judas.Death FAQ.

Moderator.View Moderator's viewpoint/theology.

NT.Dating Information on authors and dates of writing of NT books.

NT.Canon Information on early canonical collections of NT books.

OnLine.Bibles List of online Bibles available.

Policy Moderator's policies for soc.religion.christian.bible-study.

Psalm.Numbering Psalm numbering guide.

Trinity A Study on the doctrine of the Trinity by Frank DeCenso.

Theologos
listserv@vax.augustana.edu
Send a one line message text (not subject line) that says:
`subscribe theologos Chris Christian`
Discussion of systematic theology.

Theonomy-L
mail-server@dlhpfm.uucp
Send a one line message text (not subject line) that says:
`subscribe theonomy-1 Chris Christian`

Discussion group centered around Theonomy, that is, the application of the law of God to society.

Visions

Visions
listserv@ubvm.cc.buffalo.edu
Send a one line message text (not subject line) that says:
subscribe visions Chris Christian
Discussion in a charitable and Christian context of dreams, visions, prophecies, and spiritual gifts.

Women

Femrel-L
listserv@mizzou1.missouri.edu
Send a one line message text (not subject line) that says:
subscribe femrel-1 Chris Christian
Discussion of feminist theology, women and religion, and women's roles in the church.

Worship

Praise Songs
http://www.crhc.uiuc.edu/~mhsiao/iccf/
songFile.html
Collection of Christian praise songs with lyrics and guitar chords.

soc.religion.christian
Moderated discussion about all aspects of the Christian faith. Topics include, but are not limited to: eschatology, worship, denominations, soteriology, evangelism, churches, and Christian culture.

Youngstown Free-Net
yfn.ysu.edu
(USA—Ohio—Youngstown Free-Net) Worship—House of Worship—Christian Religion

Worship
worship-request@uiuc.edu
Send a one line message text (not subject line) that says:
subscribe worship christian@church.org
to the above address and put your Internet address in place of christian@church.org.
A discussion group centered around encouraging one another to worship in the way mentioned in John 4:23. Topics include philosophy of worship, questions, concerns, experiences, and practical suggestions.

Youth

Alachua County Freenet (Family Explorer)
http://www.freenet.edu/ht-
free.famexpl.html
A bulletin of activities for adults to do with children for learning about science and the environment. Although there are often Christian leanings, it is a secular publication.

alt.org.royal-rangers
Unmoderated newsgroup about the Royal Rangers, an Assemblies of God youth program.

Camp Redcloud
http://www.sccsi.com/Redcloud/home.html
Information about Camp Redcloud, a Christian conference center and youth camp located in Colorado.

1 Corinthians 2:2 Home Page
http://www.cs.indiana.edu/hyplan/
jstogdil.html
Home page serving several Christian groups, particularly focused toward high school and college students. Features include several youth groups and an online newsletter.

Lutheran Homepage
http://www.maths.tcd.ie/hyplan/thomas/
lutheran/page.html
Developed by a student with a focus on the Evangelical Lutheran Church in America and Lutheranism in general. References include *Luther's Small Catechism* and the Athanasian Creed, as well as ELCA youth and general activities and information.

MKNet
http://www.calvin.edu/~heknat/mknet/
mknet.html
Web page for Missionary kids.

MKNet
mknet-request@calvin.edu
Send a one line subject line that says: "subscribe" (without the quotes)
Mailing list for Missionary Kids (MKs) and those interested in MKs to encourage one another and share in the unique struggles of being an MK.

Royal Rangers Web Page
http://www.rahul.net/rangers/
A home page associated with the Royal Rangers, a world-wide ministry to reach boys for Christ started by the Assemblies of God Church. Information about the ministry and how to join is found here.

Soc.Religion.Christian.Youth-Work
youth-work@ucs.orst.edu
Send a one line message text (not subject line) that says:
subscribe christian@church.org
to the above address and put your Internet address in place of christian@church.org.
E-mail version of the soc.religion.christian.youth-work USENET group. If you subscribe to this list, you will receive everything posted to the newsgroup.

soc.religion.christian.youth-work
Moderated discussion about ministry to young people. Christians involved in youth work are encouraged to share stories, struggles, prayer requests, resources, suggestions, and anything else that could assist another in that ministry.

Soc.Religion.Christian.Youth-Work Web Page
http://www.engr.orst.edu:80/~freilish/youth-work.html
A Web site associated with the soc.religion.christian.youth-work newsgroup. It features ideas for activities, Bible studies, and missions work and provides a place for prayer requests and announcements.

Teen Mania
http://www.ksu.edu/~airforc/tmpix.html
Web page about Teen Mania missions organization. Information about conferences and mission trips are available.

Youth with a Mission International
http://www.xs4all.nl:80/~gwb/YWAM/
Web page introducing YWAM and their missions activities.

Glossary of Cyberspace Terms

analog—A continuous wave-like signal, such as speech and music.

anonymous FTP—A type of File Transfer Protocol that permits public access files.

ANSI—American National Standards Institute. Terminal setting required for some bulletin board systems.

AOL—America Online. A commercial on-line service.

Archie— A search utility used to find files on anonymous FTP sites.

ARPA—Advanced Research Projects Agency. The original developer of the Internet.

ASCII—American Standard Code for Information Interchange. The command to set the FTP transfer type to exchange a text file.

backbone—A series of high-speed connections upon which a computer network is built.

bandwidth—The measurement of how much information can be transmitted through a line in a given period of time.

baud rate—A term, often incorrectly used to mean bits per second, which measures the frequency of an electronic transmission.

BB—Bulletin board. Same as BBS.

BBS—Bulletin board system. An online computer system that allows the exchange of mail, message posting, and file downloading.

binary—The command to set the FTP transfer type to exchange a non–text program.

bit—The smallest unit of information used by a computer.

BITNET—Because It's Time Network. A North American network for research and education.

bounced mail—An e-mail message that is returned to the sender, usually due to an error in the destination address.

bps—Bits per second. The measurement of a modem's speed or throughput. Common rates include 2400, 9600, and 14,400.

browser—An interface program, such as Mosaic and Lynx, that allows access to the World Wide Web.

byte—The basic computer information unit, equal to one character, which consists of eight bits.

CD-ROM—Compact Disc-Read Only Memory. A high capacity optical storage medium.

CIM—CompuServe Information Manager. A graphical interface for CompuServe.

CIN—Christian Interactive Network. A Premium service offered by CompuServe.

CIS—CompuServe Information System. A commercial online service.

CIX—Commercial Internet Exchange. A TCP/IP network developed to permit commercial and business use of the Internet.

client—A computer that requests information from a server.

cyberspace—A term used to describe the electronic world that exists outside of physical space. Cyberspace was coined by William Gibson in his novel *Neuromancer*.

dedicated line—A continually active direct connection between two computers.

dial-up—A type of computer connection made on-demand using a modem.

digital—A noncontinuous signal consisting of finite values, such as a computer signal.

domain name—The part of an Internet address to the right of the @ used to identify an Internet-attached computer system.

DOS—Disk Operating System. An operating system bundled with most IBM-compatible personal computers.

DOSCIM—DOS CompuServe Information Manager. A graphical interface for CompuServe used on DOS platforms.

download—To electronically retrieve a file from a remote computer to a local one.

e-mail—Electronic mail.

e-text—Electronic text. Often refers to electronic versions of articles or books.

e-zine—Electronic magazine.

Elm—A UNIX mailer.

emoticon—An arrangement of characters meant to convey feelings. For instance, 8-) is a smiley face.

FAQ—Frequently Asked Questions. A list of common questions and answers, often posted to a USENET group.

Fidonet—A network of computer bulletin board systems.

Finger—A command to inquire about another Internet user.

flame—A hostile, nasty electronic message. Usually a response to an inappropriate post.

flame war—When multiple users flame one another.

forum—A topical discussion group.

FTP—File Transfer Protocol. A means of sending and receiving documents and programs over the Internet.

gateway—An electronic pipeline between different computer networks.

GIF—Graphic Interchange Format. A picture format common to many online graphics and digitized photos.

Gopher—A menu-based tool used to navigate the Internet.

GUI—Graphical User Interface.

hardware—A computer and associated peripherals.

hard drive—A hardware component where computer software is stored.

home page—A World Wide Web document containing text, graphics, sound, video, or hypertext links.

host—A computer system.

HTML—Hypertext Markup Language. A specification used to develop World Wide Web home pages.

HTTP—Hypertext Transfer Protocol. A specification used to exchange information within the World Wide Web.

hypertext—A means of linking information based on key words or topics.

hytelnet—A menu-driven Telnet program.

inline image—A graphic displayed on a World Wide Web home page.

Internet—An international computer network (actually, a network of networks) based on the TCP/IP protocol.

IP—Internet Protocol.

IP address—The address of a computer connected to the Internet. IP addresses are typically in a dotted decimal format such as 144.195.4.13.

Kermit—A communications protocol used for file transfer between computers.

LAN—Local Area Network. A computer network typically limited in size to a single building or floor.

listserv—An automated mailing list processor. Also a generic term for an electronic mailing list.

log in—The act of connecting to an online service by entering your username and password.

log off—The act of disconnecting from an online service.

log on—Same as log in.

lurk—The act of following a discussion, typically on USENET, without contributing anything.

Lynx—A text-only World Wide Web interface found on many UNIX systems.

Mac—Apple Macintosh.

MacOS—The Macintosh Operating System.

MacCIM—Macintosh CompuServe Information Manager. A graphical interface for CompuServe used on Apple Macintosh platforms.

MacTCP—A common TCP/IP package for the Mac.

mailer—A program which allows a user to send, receive, read, and store electronic mail messages.

mailing list—A topical discussion held through e-mail.

meg—Megabyte.

megabyte—1024 bytes. A common measure of computer memory.

megahertz—A measurement of speed equivalent to 1024 processor cycles per second.

MHz—Megahertz.

modem—Modulator-demodulator. A hardware peripheral which allows computers to communicate through a phone line.

moderator—A user who ensures that a newsgroup or mailing list stays on topic.

Mosaic—A graphical World Wide Web browser, often used as a generic term for any graphical Web browser.

multimedia—The computer use of sound, graphics, and video. A multimedia computer often comes equipped with a sound card and CD-ROM drive.

NcFTP—A user-friendly FTP interface that automates anonymous FTP connections.

netiquette—Network Etiquette. The rules of etiquette that govern USENET.

NetNews—Same as USENET.

Netscape—A commercial Web browser.

network—Multiple computers connected together for the purpose of exchanging information.

newsreader—A program which allows a user to subscribe to groups, read messages, and post responses on USENET.

newsgroup—A topical discussion group found on USENET.

newbie—A new user of the Internet.

NIC—Network Information Center. The organization responsible for managing IP addresses and domain names of computers on the Internet.

NNTP—Network News Transport Protocol. A protocol specifying how computers exchange USENET postings.

NSFnet—National Science Foundation Network. A high-speed network backbone developed during the 1980s.

offline—A system that has disconnected from a remote computer.

online—A system that is connected to a remote computer. Generic term, like cyberspace, used to describe the electronic world.

OS/2—Operating System/2. IBM's advanced operating system for personal computers.

packet—An electronic envelope containing information to be sent over the Internet.

PC—Personal Computer. Typically used to refer to IBM-compatible systems.

Pine—A UNIX mailer recommended for beginners.

plan—A message that is displayed when an account is Fingered.

posting—The act of placing a message on a USENET group.

postmaster—A person responsible for all electronic mail issues at a particular site.

PowerMac—Apple Macintosh that uses the PowerPC processor chip.

PPP—Point to Point Protocol. A TCP/IP protocol used for dial-up Internet connections. Considered to be the replacement for SLIP.

processor—A chip that serves as the engine of a computer.

protocol—A specification dictating how computer systems communicate with each other.

RAM—Random Access Memory. The area where a computer stores data during processing.

server—A computer that provides information to client computers upon request.

Shareware—Software offered on a "try before you buy" philosophy.

shell—A UNIX system interface.

SIG—Special Interest Group. A topical discussion group.

signature block—A section at the bottom of an e-mail message or USENET posting which identifies the author.

SLIP—Serial Line Internet Protocol. A TCP/IP protocol used for dial-up Internet connections.

SMTP—Simple Mail Transfer Protocol. The TCP/IP protocol which specifies how electronic mail is transferred.

snail-mail—The United States Postal Service.

software—The programs that run on a computer.

sound card—A hardware peripheral which enables a computer to produce high-quality sound.

spamming—The act of posting multiple copies of a message to inappropriate USENET groups.

Sysop—System Operator. A user who manages a computer bulletin board or computer system.

TCP/IP—Transmission Control Protocol/ Internet Protocol. A suite of computer protocols which dictate how computers exchange information over the Internet.

TCP/IP Stack—Software implementation of the TCP/IP protocol which allows a personal computer to connect to the Internet via SLIP/PPP.

Telnet—A means of connecting to a nonlocal computer on the Internet.

terminal emulator—A software package that allows computers to communicate using a modem.

thread—A discussion topic within a USENET group.

Tin—A UNIX USENET newsreader recommended for beginners.

Trn—A UNIX USENET newsreader.

trolling—The act of posting a hostile or factually incorrect message to a USENET group with the intent of starting a flame war or eliciting meaningless chatter.

type—An extension found in an Internet e-mail address to identify the originating location. Common types include `.edu` for educational institutions and `.com` for commercial entities.

UNIX—A computer operating system developed by Bell Laboratories.

upload—To electronically send a file from a local computer to a remote one.

URL—Uniform Resource Locator. A standard addressing method which identifies information on the Internet; used when navigating the World Wide Web.

USENET—A series of topical discussion groups found on the Internet. Groups are arranged in a hierarchical fashion with dotted names such as `rec.music.christian`.

username—An individual's account name on a computer system.

UUCP—UNIX to UNIX Copy Protocol. A protocol used to exchange files.

Veronica—Very Easy Rodent-Oriented Netwide Index to Computerized Archives. A search utility for Gopher.

virus—A computer program that can be transferred between computers, often causing harm.

VT100—A common terminal emulation setting for text-based communications.

W3—World Wide Web.

WAIS—Wide Area Information Server. A method of indexing documents by key word, often used with Gopher.

WAN—Wide Area Network. A computer network which encompasses a large geographic area.

Web browser—An interface program, such as Mosaic and Lynx, that enables access to the World Wide Web.

whois—A command that searches a list of Internet usernames and domain names in order to locate an individual or organization.

WinCIM—Windows CompuServe Information Manager. A graphical interface for CompuServe used on Windows platforms.

Windows—Microsoft's operating system for IBM-compatible personal computers.

Winsock—Windows Socket. A TCP/IP implementation for IBM compatible computers running Windows.

World Wide Web—An Internet tool which enables users to explore the Internet using hypertext links.

WWW—World Wide Web.

Xmodem—A communications protocol used for file transfer between computers.

Ymodem—A communications protocol used for file transfer between computers.

Zine—Electronic magazine.

Zmodem—A communications protocol used for file transfer between computers.

About the Author

Jason D. Baker is an educational consultant at Loyola College in Maryland. A Bucknell University graduate in electrical engineering, he has been an active cyberspace citizen for over ten years. He has published a number of articles related to the use of computer technology in the building of God's kingdom. Jason and his wife, Julianne, live in Baltimore.

Christian Cyberspace Companion addresses a rapidly growing and changing environment. In order to better serve the Christian community, your feedback would be greatly appreciated. How has this book helped you navigate in the online world? What would make the book easier or more useful? What other topics should be addressed? What resources should be added, deleted, or modified in the Christian BBS List or Christian Internet Directory? All suggestions are welcome.

I hope you find this adventure as exciting as I have. Please feel free to drop me a note once you get online. You can reach me at the *CCC* Web page located at **http://www.bakerbooks.com/ccc/** or by e-mail at **jdb@loyola.edu**. I look forward to hearing from you.